FAST, FRESH
GARI
EDIBLES

CRE▲TIVE
HOMEOWNER®

FAST, FRESH
GARDEN
EDIBLES

Quick Crops
for Small Spaces

JANE COURTIER

First Published in North America in 2011 by
CREATIVE HOMEOWNER®
Upper Saddle River, NJ 07458

CREATIVE
HOMEOWNER®

Toucan Books
Design: Nick Avery Design
Editor: Theresa Bebbington
Managing Editor: Ellen Dupont
Picture Research: Sharon Southren
Picture Manager: Christine Vincent
Indexer: Marie Lorimer
Proofreader: Constance Novis

Creative Homeowner
VP/Publisher: Timothy O. Bakke
Art Director: David Geer
Managing Editor: Fran J. Donegan
Production Coordinator: Sara M. Markowitz
Digital Imaging Specialist: Mary Dolan

10 9 8 7 6 5 4 3 2 1

Fast, Fresh Garden Edibles, First Edition
Library of Congress Control Number: 2010932140
ISBN-10: 1-58011-512-8
ISBN-13: 978-1-58011-512-4

CREATIVE HOMEOWNER®
A Division of Federal Marketing Corp.
24 Park Way
Upper Saddle River, NJ 07458
www.creativehomeowner.com

Disclaimer: The author and publishers have made every effort to ensure
that all the instructions given in this book are safe and accurate, but they
cannot accept liability for any resulting injuries or loss or damage to either
property or person, whether direct or consequential and howsoever arising.
Be sure to familiarize yourself with manufacturer's instructions for tools,
equipment, and materials before beginning a project.

Planet Friendly Publishing
✓ Made in the United States
✓ Printed on Recycled Paper
Text: 10%   Cover: 10%
Learn more: www.greenedition.org

GREEN
EDITION

At Creative Homeowner we're committed to
producing books in an earth-friendly manner and to
helping our customers make greener choices.

Manufacturing books in the United States ensures
compliance with strict environmental laws and
eliminates the need for international freight shipping,
a major contributor to global air pollution.

And printing on recycled paper helps minimize our
consumption of trees, water, and fossil fuels. *Fast,
Fresh Garden Edibles* was printed on paper made
with 10% post-consumer waste. According to the
Environmental Defense Fund Paper Calculator, by
using this innovative paper instead of conventional
papers we achieved the following environmental
benefits:

Trees Saved: 29

Water Saved: 13,433 gallons

Solid Waste Eliminated: 816 pounds

Greenhouse Gas Emissions Eliminated:
2,789 pounds

For more information on our environmental
practices, please visit us online at
www.creativehomeowner.com/green

Contents

The need for speed

Growing your own food can be one of the most satisfying and rewarding forms of gardening. Yet, nature doesn't usually produce instant results, and many gardeners are generally willing to wait to reap what they have sown. However, there are also many potential gardeners who would grow their own vegetables if only they knew they could get faster results. The good news is they can.

Can't wait, won't wait

Many people live in a speed-obsessed world these days. They grumble if the Internet takes more than a few seconds to connect, and the idea of traveling to the other side of the world in a matter of hours doesn't raise an eyebrow. Perhaps it's not surprising that people are eager to get speedier harvests from their vegetable gardens.

It's not just that we're impatient. Most people tend to have busy lives, whether it's due to working long hours, too many family commitments, or enjoying some of the many leisure activities that are now available. While dedicated gardeners consider gardening to be their major hobby and enjoy spending many hours engrossed in it, others are not so committed. Yes, they enjoy a little gardening if it fits into their schedule, but there are other demands on their time that, for them, are just as important. For these people, *Fast, Fresh Garden Edibles* is the ideal book, providing ways to bring the pleasure of growing vegetables— and some fruits and herbs, too—into a busy lifestyle, even if it means cutting a few corners here and there.

Fast food—only the best

Fortunately, there are many vegetables that produce great results. Food that is grown fast is not just more satisfying for people in a hurry but is often of a better quality, too. Many types of vegetables don't need a long season in which to mature and develop their flavor. Instead, they are at their most succulent, tender, and tasty when you harvest them while still young. "Baby" vegetables are sold in most grocery stores, and the public is willing to pay a premium price for what is considered to be a premium product.

There are also vegetables that may not be the quickest candidates, from sowing or transplanting to harvest, but once the vegetables are in the ground, you can—almost—forget about them until they are ready for picking. (For more on which vegetables to choose, see "Picking the Winners," pages 72–167.)

Lost the plot

You don't even need to have a vegetable plot to grow vegetables. There is such a huge variety of vegetables from which to choose that you'll be able to find some suitable for growing mixed with flowers in a border, others in a raised bed on your patio, and even those that will thrive in pots and other containers on a balcony. (See pages 16 through 29.)

Making things easier

As far as this book is concerned, "fast food" doesn't just mean vegetables that you can harvest within a short time of planting or sowing. The vegetables are often easy to grow because they don't require complicated, time-consuming cultivation techniques.

The main secret of getting plants to grow fast is to provide them with ideal growing conditions, which is often easier than it may seem. (See "Get Ready to Grow,"

pages 30–71.) In a nutshell, this usually means making sure the soil is broken down to a fine, crumbly texture to let roots spread through it rapidly. Once you have sown or transplanted the plants, you then need to provide them with ample supplies of moisture, both at the roots and in the atmosphere. The plants will also need to receive sufficient quantities of the right nutrients for fast growth. Finally, you need to keep plants at their optimum growing temperature, without too many fluctuations. Plants have different requirements, so you will have to know what conditions to provide for your various vegetables. (See "Picking the Winners," pages 72–167.)

Once you understand how to acheive these basics, you will be on course for success. You may need to invest a small amount of time and energy up front to get the soil ready, but then you will need to provide only minimum effort during the growing season. It will be a matter of weeks—and in some cases even only a few days—before you'll be harvesting your own fast, fresh vegetables.

Opposte: A small raised bed is easy to maintain, making it suitable for the busy person. It's also a great way to provide growing space where there isn't available ground in a yard.

Above: After the initial soil preparation, a small vegetable plot often needs just a little time each week for planting, care, and harvesting.

Where does your garden grow?

You don't need a large yard to grow vegetables. Even the tiniest yard can provide enough room for a reasonable crop. What if you have room for only a few containers? You can still grow vegetables, as long as you can be creative with your space to provide the plants with what they need.

Making plans

No matter what size your outdoor space, you can grow some vegetables and herbs, even if it is just a chili or a few herbs on a windowsill. If you have only a small yard—or even no yard at all—you might be surprised at how much you can still produce.

Suburban yards have been growing steadily smaller over the years. As the price of land—along with the size of the population—increases, it makes economic sense for house builders to squeeze as many homes in a given area as they can, and that often means less outdoor space for everyone. Fewer people today have the luxury of keeping a vegetable patch separate from an ornamental flower garden. For those living in urban areas, apartments that come with any type of outdoor space attached, such as a courtyard, are scarce. One option can be to get involved in a community garden.

Below: A white background will help reflect light onto plants, including those, such as these tomatoes, in planters hung on the walls.

Right: Urban gardeners are adept at using roof spaces for vegetable gardening, but they need to make sure the structure is strong enough to support the weight of the fully planted pots.

Making space

Having little or no outdoor space doesn't mean that you have no room for food crops. In the same way that fast-growing, easy-care vegetables don't require as much of your time as you might have expected, fruits and vegetables don't need that much space. Don't just look at the obvious areas of ground space for growing your vegetables. You can grow plants in pots on balconies, on windowsills, and at the sides of paths and steps. Walls and fences can support climbers and scramblers, as well as hanging baskets.

If you are planning a roof garden or intend to grow vegetables on your balcony, be sure that the structures will support the weight of the plants and soil in pots, and that hanging baskets and window boxes are safely secured, especially if they are up high.

Once you've decided on a space, the next step is to look at the conditions. You may need to improve or adapt them before you can start growing your own vegetables.

Light and shade

Fruit and vegetable plants like good, bright light; they will struggle to grow well in shade. Most yards are shady only in certain areas or at certain times of the day. On a sunny day, take photographs of your yard or outdoor space every two or three hours so that you have a record of exactly which areas are shaded and for how long. This will help you decide the best position for your vegetables.

If your urban outdoor space is shaded by high walls or fences, you can improve the quality of light by painting their surfaces white or a light color or by propping a reflective or light-colored material against them. Prune back trees and shrubs that are casting shade; however, if a neighbor's tree is causing the shade, first ask for permission.

Mini weather patterns

The climate of your outdoor space will obviously depend on its geographical location, and your local Cooperative Extension Service can help provide information about your area's growing conditions. However, within any locale there are also microclimates to take into account. Outdoor spaces in urban locations are usually warmer than those in rural areas because of the heat given off by the surrounding buildings. They may also be sheltered from frost and cold winds. The average date of the last frost in your outdoor space can also vary from your neighbor's. Cold air will sink and roll downhill, so if you live at the bottom of a slope, you may find you are not safely frost free until some days after your neighbor's yard at the top of the hill.

You can use walls, fences, hedges, and screens to improve the climate in areas of your yard and make it more suitable for growing vegetables. In addition to sheltering plants from cold and wind, in hot regions they can enable you to grow cool-season crops by providing shade, which lowers the temperature and protects foliage from the damaging heat of the sun.

Where's the water?

Small vegetable gardens, especially those with a lot of plants in containers, usually require a lot of watering during the summer months. An outside faucet will make life much easier than struggling to fill watering cans at the kitchen sink, and if you can, installing one will be a time-saving investment. Where a yard is completely paved, make sure excess water has somewhere to safely drain away—without causing a problem for your neighbors.

Above: Small containers are easy to move from a shady to a sunny area, and some vegetables, such as Swiss chard, can fit in easily with typical ornamental plants.

Below: Tall planters and high raised beds make harvesting vegetables easier for those with aching joints or limited mobility.

The lowdown

You don't need to be an expert in botany to grow good vegetables, but a basic knowledge of how plants develop will help you get the best results from your vegetables.

Life on the earth depends on plants—we cannot exist without them. Green plants have the unique ability to convert energy from sunlight into food. The carbohydrates that are produced by this process (which is known as photosynthesis) not only fuel the plants' own needs but also provide the basic food source for all animals in the food chain.

The structure of plants

Plant life takes many different forms—you have only to look around any yard to see that. There is a huge variety among vegetables in the size, shape, stems, and leaves of the plants. Left to nature, the process of natural selection often results in only the most efficient plant forms surviving. However, over thousands of years, farmers and growers have intervened, selecting and nurturing particular variations that suit their own purposes. The result is the fantastic variety of plants that is available to us today. Even so, virtually all plants have some features in common.

Roots

A tiny root is usually the first part of the plant to emerge from a germinating seed. The pull of gravity sends roots growing downward, and on most plants they branch and spread widely, anchoring the plant firmly in place. Their job is to absorb water and minerals from the soil, which they do through tiny, fragile hairs on the root tips. Careless transplanting of vegetables that damages the root tips will usually have a negative impact on the plants because it destroys part of their water-gathering network. However, if the damage is not too extensive, the roots will swiftly regrow. In some plants, roots also swell to form a food-storage organ, and people take advantage of this in the case of root crops, such as turnips and beets.

Shoots

Unlike roots, shoots grow against gravity, emerging from a germinating seed in the soil into the daylight. The shoots grow in different forms. They may be upright, branching stems, such as those of tomatoes and kale, or they may form a low rosette of leaves, as in the case of lettuce, which only produces a recognizable stem when it flowers. Other plants, such as pole beans and zucchini, produce climbing or scrambling stems; still others, such as onions and kohlrabi, have swollen stems used for food storage. These swollen stems are often confused with roots, particularly when underground, as in the case of potato tubers.

Leaves

Photosynthesis mainly takes place in the leaves. Most leaves have a large surface area in relation to their size to absorb the maximum amount of light, but their shapes vary a great deal. Leaves are given their green color by a substance called "chlorophyll," which is needed for photosynthesis. Some leaves do not appear green, such as those of red beets; however, they still contain chlorophyll, although its green color is masked.

Flowers

The reproductive part of the plant is the flower, where seeds are formed for a new generation. Some vegetables, such as tomatoes, peas, beans, and zucchini, are grown specifically for their fruit and seeds. On these plants, gardeners can encourage the formation of flowers and make sure they are pollinated to ensure that fruit production takes place. Other vegetables, such as broccoli, are grown for their immature flower buds, and pollination is not relevant. Conversely, with some vegetables, flowering is a nuisance that gardeners try to avoid. When plants such as lettuce and spinach start to flower, it ruins their leafy crop.

Beet roots

Pea shoots

Kale leaves

Zucchini flowers

What plants need

Understanding what your plants require to grow well is important to achieving a good-quality crop. Different types of fruits and vegetables need different conditions, but all plants share some basic requirements. While plants can perform the magic trick of making food out of fresh air and sunlight, they do need a few props to pull this off with the most success.

Soil and nutrients

A plant needs a firm base in which to anchor itself so that it can grow. This growing medium needs to be of the right texture for the roots to penetrate and spread through it easily, and it must hold enough moisture for the roots to absorb. (See "Ground Rules," pages 32–33.) In most cases, the growing medium is soil, either natural soil from the garden or a packaged product. Potting mix available from garden centers is usually a soilless mix based on peat or a peat substitute, plus plant nutrients. You can also buy soil-based mixes made from sterilized garden soil. (See "Planting Your Containers," pages 48–49.)

The minerals that plants need are supplied by the growing medium. If gardeners want stronger, larger crops, they can supplement

Water

Water is important for plants. Water pressure within the cells keeps plants firm and upright, preventing them from wilting. All the minerals needed must be dissolved in water before plants can transport and make use of them, and water is essential for photosynthesis, the process by which plants manufacture their source of energy. The natural source of water for plants is rain, but in some areas there is not enough rainfall for growing certain vegetables. Urban gardens surrounded by tall buildings often receive a limited amount of rain. For plants being grown in containers, where the amount of soil is restricted, natural rainfall is rarely sufficient. (See "Watering," pages 50–51.)

Annual, biennial, or perennial

Plants that germinate, grow, produce seeds, and die within a year are known as annuals. Biennials germinate and grow in one year and then flower in the next. Perennials survive the winters and continue to grow and produce a crop for a number of years. Most of the vegetables that gardeners grow are annuals, or they are biennials or perennials treated as annuals by harvesting them before they mature. However, a few vegetables, such as globe artichokes, and fruits, such as blueberries, are grown as perennials.

the natural supply by adding fertilizers. (See "Food for Thought," pages 54–55.)

Warmth

Plants need warmth to start photosynthesizing and growing, but the amount of warmth they prefer varies from one species to another. In general, temperatures at 65–80°F (18–27°C) produce the best results, but adjust your planting and sowing dates according to your climate. (See "Hardiness and Heat Zones," pages 34–35.)

You can extend the growing season by starting seeds indoors and planting them outdoors when warm enough, or by using covers. (See "Vegetables for Transplanting," pages 42–43, and "Going under Cover," pages 58–59.)

Air and light

Carbon dioxide and oxygen from the air are essential for photosynthesis and respiration, but they are unlikely to be in short supply. However, allowing good movement of air around plants is essential because stagnant, moist air encourages fungal diseases, such as damping off and botrytis. Growing plants at the correct spacing, and thinning them out early, will help to keep them healthy, as will removing weeds competing for space. (See "Weeding Out the Competition," pages 60–61.)

Plants convert light to energy, so they need a good source of light to grow well. Heavily shaded areas rarely grow good vegetables and fruits. Some light or dappled shade for part of the day is not a problem; in fact, it can be valuable in some climates where strong sun can scorch leaves in the hottest part of the day.

Opposite left: Lettuce is just one of the vegetables that will wilt quickly if not provided with adequate amounts of water.

Opposite top: A fine, crumbly texture will make it easier for the roots of seedlings and transplants to spread through the soil.

Above: When choosing a vegetable gardening area, make sure it will receive plenty of sunlight.

Left: Tomatoes are one of the warm-season crops, along with squash and peppers, that love the heat. In most regions, start these indoors and wait until warm weather before planting outside. Start cool-season vegetables, such as radish, spinach, and turnips, directly outdoors.

Small spaces, big ideas

Don't let limited outdoor space make you think you can't grow your own food—there's always space for a vegetable of some kind. Take a look at the small growing spaces here—and at the ideas on the following pages—to provide inspiration for your own situation.

Above: A vegetable patch doesn't need to be huge. This small, informal plot provides plenty of space for beans, carrots, and beets, among other vegetables.

Your options will depend on your living accommodation. You may have a yard in which you can dedicate a small section for a patch, or you might be able to fit vegetables in with ornamental plantings in a flower bed or border. Perhaps you can use a patio, deck, balcony, or roof space for growing vegetables. Even if these are not options for you, a window can be enough for fresh herbs, salad greens, and perhaps even a few sweet peppers.

The first step is to look at the space you have with an open mind. Any experienced gardener with a small yard knows that you have to make every inch count. By using some typical gardening techniques and adapting them in innovative ways, you can grow your own vegetables in small spaces.

The space race

Not having any outdoor space does not mean all is lost. Windows come to the rescue here. You can position a hanging basket indoors near a sunny window using a ceiling hook or wall bracket. Planters filled with herbs and compact, short-rooted vegetables are also an option for a sunny window that has a wide ledge or on a table near it. Outdoor window boxes are a third option. However, if you live above the first-floor level, make sure the window box is securely attached to the wall.

Balconies are a real boon, providing outdoor growing space even in a high-rise apartment building. Planters, window boxes, and hanging baskets are all good choices. Consider using hanging baskets with a pulley system to raise and lower the planters for watering and harvesting.

The weight of soil-filled containers may limit the size and number of containers you can use. If you're not sure of the safety of your balcony, have a structural engineer survey it. Always make sure outdoor containers on a balcony are safe, without any danger of being knocked to the ground.

As long as they get some sun for at least part of the day, these can be ideal places to grow plants in containers; tender vegetables, such as peppers and tomatoes, will thrive in the sheltered conditions. Walls and paving absorb heat from the sun during the day and gradually release it over several hours, meaning that a sheltered patio or courtyard can remain several degrees warmer than the surrounding area into the night. It will protect plants from frost and chilling winds, giving you heavier and earlier crops.

It may be possible to lift an area of paving to expose some soil underneath, or you can build a raised bed directly on top of the paving. Raised beds allow you to try a wider range of plants than you can grow in pots.

If you do have a yard with ground space, you may still need to juggle the needs of other family members, too. While you might be happy to turn the entire yard over to food production, others might be more interested in creating a peaceful area for relaxing, having lawn space for children, or growing ornamental plants. With a little careful planning, your vegetables can find a space without taking over, and you will achieve a compromise that pleases everyone.

Left: Vertical structures are a great way of making extra space for growing vegetables.

Below: A courtyard garden is an ideal space for plants. Even if there's no soil, you can build raised beds for growing vegetables.

Up on the roof

A roof garden can be a wonderful oasis, providing the same options as a balcony. However, if you plan to make one, first be sure the roof is strong enough to support the weight. Even when using lightweight containers and a soilless mix, freshly watered plants in pots can be heavy. As with a balcony, a structural engineer can advise you whether your roof area is structurally safe.

At ground level

For some homes, the outdoor space is just a small patio area, completely paved over, with no soil in which to grow plants. Often these small plots are courtyards, surrounded with walls or fences.

No garden, no **problem**

Even in a home with no outdoor ground space, one can usually find a place for a few containers. As long as there is reasonable light, porches, steps, and walkways can all be pressed into use, and in these situations, pots, window boxes, and hanging baskets come into their own.

Up in the air

Hanging baskets can be used for growing a large range of vegetable plants and herbs, and baskets with several tiers make fantastic use of space (left). Be careful that you position them where the overspill from watering will not cause a problem. It goes without saying that they need to be firmly secured to their supports.

Retro chic

A little space near the door provides the perfect spot for one or two containers (right). Here, a couple of pieces of recycled kitchen equipment—an old enamel bucket and flour container—add a retro-style touch as containers for a tomato plant and some beans. Just be sure that unusual containers have enough drainage to keep the vegetable plants from becoming waterlogged.

On the window

Windows are ideal places to grow vegetables, particularly when they are in full sun (above). Make them a decorative feature by choosing exterior window boxes in attractive materials, such as this woven willow. Window brackets should be securely bolted to the walls, with the planter firmly secured to the brackets.

Keep it cropping

Cut-and-come-again plants, such as these beet leaves (below), are ideal for small spaces, and you can keep the plants going for several weeks in the same pots. A sunroom or a table near a sunny window is a great space for growing plants.

Walk this way

This combined planting of dill and bush beans (above) is tucked at the edge of a walkway. Paths and steps often make useful spots for containers, but keep in mind that poorly placed pots on frequently used thoroughfares can be a hazard for people passing by, particularly if the pots are in poorly lit areas that will be used after dark.

No garden, no problem
continued

Pack them in

Where space is tight, cram together as many plants in as many different containers as you can. This corner (left) contains a lively combination of vegetables, including tomatoes, peas, and cut-and-come-again lettuce, among others, all held together by the central feature of bright, tumbling nasturtium flowers.

Take it easy

An open porch or veranda is a delightful place to sit and relax, surrounded by the fruits of your labor (right). The fragrance of herbs and warm aroma of ripening tomatoes can be just as pleasurable as the scent from flowers, particularly when you know you can reach out and pluck your lunchtime salad from your seat.

New dimensions

With a little imagination, you can find new places to display plants. Use new dimensions to add vitality to a small area. Planters and stands, as well as plants, can provide color and interest. Here, painted steps (right) provide a vertical space for the plants, while the deep blue color makes an eye-catching contrast to sparkling white gravel, a perfect backdrop for when the colorful strawberries and peppers appear.

The casual touch

This bench (above) is packed with a cheerful collection of pots that is not only productive but attractive, too. A mixture of different colors of salad greens, a variety of contrasting foliage shapes, and the bright pink pompoms of chive flowers all combine to create a casual but pleasing effect.

Against the wall

The warmth from house walls (right) makes them a good place for growing plants, and this tiered bench makes the most of the space available. Vertical surfaces are often neglected in larger yards, but you can use them to the full where space is limited.

Plantings for a
courtyard garden

Your courtyard garden may be completely paved over and surrounded by walls, but don't let that deter you from growing your own food. You can use every inch of space, including the vertical surfaces, to grow a range of delicious and beautiful vegetables and fruits. Raised beds and containers can provide perfect growing conditions.

Air rights

The smaller your growing area, the more important it is to grow crops that will provide the maximum return for minimum ground space. Climbing pole beans are perfect for the courtyard (right); if they are well fed and watered, they will continue to provide regular harvests of beans all summer long.

Hanging baskets

These planters provide a new visual dimension for the garden scene and add valuable extra growing space. Trailing plants are particularly appropriate for baskets; there are a lot of tomato types specially bred for basket growing (above). Add moisture-retaining granules to the potting mix to cut down the amount of watering needed.

Cover up

Walled areas are several degrees warmer than unprotected sites, so you can produce early crops. To speed things up even more, use cloches to add a little extra protection to the most tender crops (above).

Raised beds

The next best thing to growing in the ground, tall raised beds (opposite bottom) provide plants more space than containers do, and you can increase the height of the beds if the plants need a greater depth. There are a lot of materials you can use to build the beds, so choose something that suits your courtyard's style.

Different planters

Let your imagination run wild when it comes to choosing planters, whether you use natural materials (left) or "found" objects. Just make sure your container is able to hold a reasonable depth of potting mix for the plants' roots. It must also have good drainage to avoid waterlogged plants; this may mean you need to make holes in the bottom of the container with an awl or power drill.

The productive patio or deck

Patios and decks may not seem like encouraging places to grow vegetables. However, paved surfaces absorb and radiate warmth from the sun, so a patio can be the perfect spot for plants. Containers will give you the opportunity to grow delicious crops on both patios and decks.

Off the ground

Raised beds can be built directly on top of a paved area (left). Filled with good-quality soil, they will provide enough depth for growing a number of plants. You can even grow root vegetables, such as carrots—if you choose short-root types— as well as climbers growing up supports. Provide plenty of drainage holes at the bottom of the raised bed walls—and a place for the water to drain.

Small is beautiful

Small areas of raised beds are quick and easy to maintain, and what could be more attractive and rewarding than these neat, weed-free rows of vegetable plants (right)? Raised beds can be decorative landscape features as well as a place to grow crops. The patio is the ideal place to relax after a day's work, and a little gentle weed pulling while admiring your crops in the evening warmth is a great way to round off the day.

Room with a view

With large, deep containers, many vegetables, and even fruit trees, will crop successfully (above). Most plants love the sheltered atmosphere of a sunny deck—and most gardeners appreciate it, too, finding it an ideal place to take a breather on a summer's day. A mixture of flowers and edible crops makes a pleasant view.

Make it easy

Beds raised to waist height (left) are ideal for gardeners who are not especially agile, cutting out the need for bending. This "tabletop" type of bed is also a suitable design for wheelchair users, enabling them to get up close to the plants. Metal hoops allow for the bed to be covered with insect-proof netting to protect against pests or with a floating row cover as protection from excessive cold or heat.

Beds, borders, and beyond

You can grow many types of vegetables in containers, but most will do even better when given the opportunity to spread their roots in the open ground. It will also mean less work for you because plants will need less watering and feeding and are usually easier to support, too.

Mix and match

If you only have a small area of open ground in your yard, you can supplement it with vegetables in containers (below). When growing plants that need supports, it is easier to drive stakes into a soil bed than it is to secure the supports to the containers, where the soil is usually not deep enough to hold them firmly.

Easy reach

You don't want to have to reach for your galoshes to pick lettuce or some herbs, so be sure you have a firm path from which you can reach your plants (above). A path of stepping-stones ensures that you can keep your feet dry, while wasting the minimum amount of growing space.

Flowers and food

Small plots have to fulfill many functions, and when you make the decision to grow some of your own food, you don't necessarily have to give up growing flowers. Here, a vegetable bed is linked to a separate flower border by a colorful fringe of blooms (above). Mixed beds, where the food plants are dotted in among the flowers, are also a successful option.

Island in a sea of green

A patch of emerald green lawn is a traditional yard feature that many people are reluctant to give up altogether, and cutting a bed or island into the lawn is a good compromise. This island, with a yellow-flowered zucchini bordered by lettuce (left), makes an attractive, decorative feature that would fit well in a formal layout.

Beds, borders, and **beyond** continued

Natural paths

You can use bark chips or other natural materials to form a path between raised beds (above). They blend in well, are relatively inexpensive, and are easy to lay. Use larger bark chips than those used for mulching because they will last longer.

Scent underfoot

Fragrant herbs are good for planting alongside paths, where their growth can spill over the edges (below). Each time the shoots are brushed past or lightly crushed underfoot, they release their delicious fragrances. The contrasting shapes, textures, and colors of herb foliage, from tiny-leaved silver thyme to spiky rosemary to dark opal basil, work well together in a small space.

Setting up boundaries

Putting a raised bed in a flower border is one way to separate the needs of your vegetables from those of ornamental plants (above). A fruit tree—or a tepee of beans, peas, or even scrambling squash vines—will add vertical interest.

Raising your game

If the soil in your yard is not especially fertile, building raised beds on top of it will allow you to add an extra depth of high-quality soil (left). The fact that the raised beds are not on a nonpermeable base, such as paving, but on open soil will ensure good drainage and improve growing conditions. Raised beds can make attractive landscaping features. With a suitable capping, the sides can easily double up as a garden seat—even if it's just somewhere to perch for a few minutes of rest while you're gardening.

Get ready
to grow

The main secret for getting vegetables to grow fast is to give them the ideal growing conditions. The first step is to be sure that the soil is broken down to a fine texture so that the roots can spread rapidly. Next, protect young transplants from shocks caused by fluctuating temperatures or handling when planted outdoors. Finally, keep the plants well watered, and give them the right nutrients. Follow these steps, and your vegetables will grow by leaps and bounds.

Ground rules

Good, fertile soil is important for the strong, healthy growth of all plants. By investing a little time up front on thorough soil preparation for your vegetables, you can prevent a plethora of problems and disappointments later. This is true whether you are growing your plants in beds of soil already in your yard, or you are filling raised beds or containers with store-bought soil or potting mix.

The ABCs of soil

From one garden to the next, the quality of the soil varies greatly, so check how your garden soil measures up before you start sowing and planting. Take a good look at what is already growing there. Is the existing plant growth lush, deep green, and healthy, or does it seem stunted, pale, and starved? Strong, healthy plant growth—even if it's only weeds—shows that you shouldn't have to worry about much. However, if the plants seem less than perfect to you, some soil improvements will probably be needed.

Start by taking a handful of moist soil and rubbing a pinch of it between your fingertips, adding a splash of water if it's dry. A gritty feeling indicates sandy soil, while a smooth, slippery, or sticky feeling indicates there is some clay content. Now squeeze the rest of the handful of soil and roll it between your palms; sandy soil falls apart, but clay soil is easy to mold into a ball that holds together.

Sandy soil warms up quickly and drains freely, but it is often low in nutrients and has trouble retaining water for plants. Soil that contains a lot of clay is usually fertile, with a good supply of plant nutrients. However, it can easily become waterlogged, can be difficult to work, and warms up slowly in spring.

Both types of soil can be vastly improved by adding garden compost and manure or bags of soil amendments that you can buy at nurseries and garden centers—anything that contains organic matter. Well-rotted organic matter acts like a sponge; it absorbs water and nutrients so that they are always available to plants in sandy soil. Organic matter breaks up sticky,

Above left: The best time to dig is in late fall, when the plot is bare. Cold weather during the winter months will help break up the roughly dug soil.

Right: Fill a raised bed with good-quality topsoil to be sure you grow healthy vegetables.

clinging clay, improving soil texture and making it easier for plant roots to penetrate (and for gardeners to dig).

Time to dig

In existing beds, break up the soil and remove all weeds; be sure to remove their roots, too. Dig as deeply as you can; using a garden fork is often easier than using a spade. Turn the soil over, and strike any lumps with the fork to break them up. The object is to break the soil down to a fine, crumbly texture that plant roots can easily explore, as well as to break up any consolidated layers below the surface.

The acid test

A pH scale is used to measure soil acidity: pH 7 is neutral, above 7 is alkaline, and below 7 is acidic. Most garden soil is either too acidic or too alkaline. If it is not adjusted, nutrient deficiencies and other problems can occur. You can check soil acidity with a home testing kit from a garden center. However, if you use a mail-order kit to send a sample to a laboratory for analysis, the lab will also give advice on how to adjust the soil if necessary.

Hardiness and **heat zones**

For success in growing vegetables, it is important to choose the varieties that will thrive in your climate. Some vegetables won't thrive if they get too cold, and others will suffer if they get too hot. You will need to know how cold and hot it can get, and when to expect the first and last frost dates in your area. Your local Cooperative Extension Service can help you learn about your area's climate, especially the frost dates, and these maps can be used as guidance, too. You will also need to know where to expect sunlight in your yard, so you know where to position the plants.

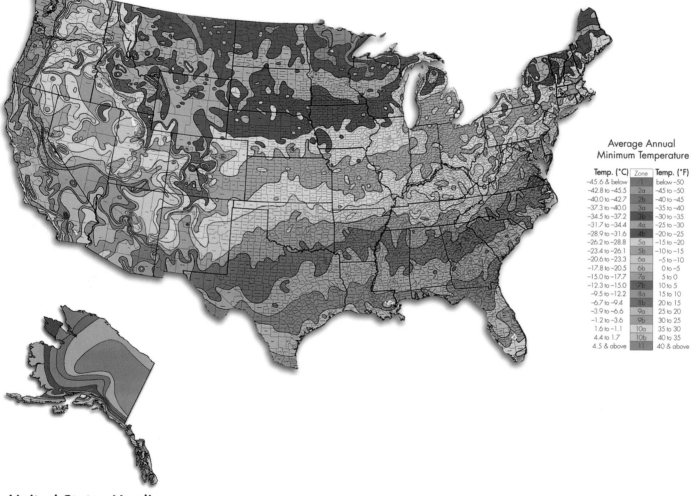

Average Annual Minimum Temperature

Temp. (°C)	Zone	Temp. (°F)
–45.6 & below	1	below –50
–42.8 to –45.5	2a	–45 to –50
–40.0 to –42.7	2b	–40 to –45
–37.3 to –40.0	3a	–35 to –40
–34.5 to –37.2	3b	–30 to –35
–31.7 to –34.4	4a	–25 to –30
–28.9 to –31.6	4b	–20 to –25
–26.2 to –28.8	5a	–15 to –20
–23.4 to –26.1	5b	–10 to –15
–20.6 to –23.3	6a	–5 to –10
–17.8 to –20.5	6b	0 to –5
–15.0 to –17.7	7a	5 to 0
–12.3 to –15.0	7b	10 to 5
–9.5 to –12.2	8a	15 to 10
–6.7 to –9.4	8b	20 to 15
–3.9 to –6.6	9a	25 to 20
–1.2 to –3.6	9b	30 to 25
1.6 to –1.1	10a	35 to 30
4.4 to 1.7	10b	40 to 35
4.5 & above	11	40 & above

United States Hardiness Zone Map

The United States Department of Agriculture (USDA) has developed a Hardiness Zone Map. In the map, various regions throughout the United States have been divided into zones based on records of the average minimum temperatures in those areas. Zone 1 has the coldest temperatures, while Zone 11 has the warmest. If you live in Zone 5, you can include plants that will thrive in Zones 1–4, too. When you buy seeds or transplants, the labels often include the hardiness zones in which the plants will survive. Within these zones, there are smaller microclimates, so you should use this information only as a guide and try experimenting.

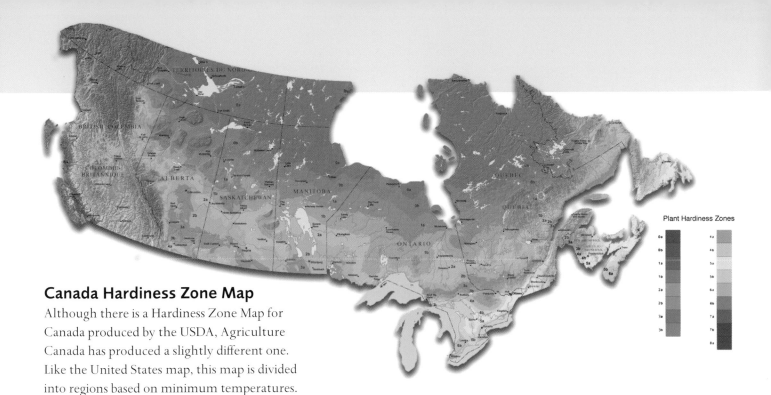

Canada Hardiness Zone Map

Although there is a Hardiness Zone Map for Canada produced by the USDA, Agriculture Canada has produced a slightly different one. Like the United States map, this map is divided into regions based on minimum temperatures.

Plant Hardiness Zones

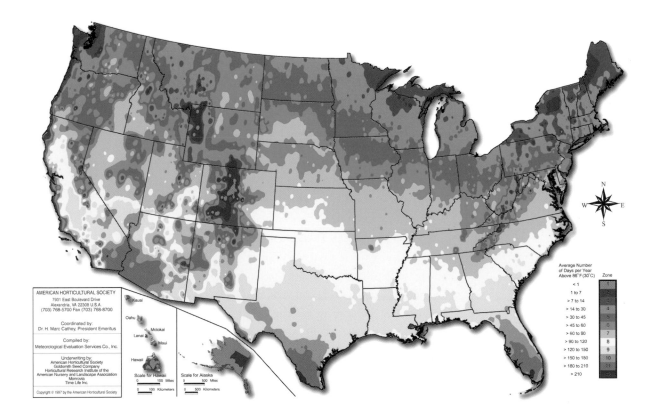

United States Heat Zone Map

The American Horticultural Society introduced their Heat Zone Map in 1998. It divides the United States into 12 zones, each one based on the average number of days over 86°F (30°C) for the region. These are known as "heat days." If you live in Zone 1, don't expect any days above 86°F (30°C), while Zone 12 will have 210 heat days in a year. Many plant breeders are now including this information in their labeling.

Sow easy

Seeds are remarkable—they contain not only an embryonic new plant but almost everything it needs to get through the first few days of life. There are few things more fascinating and satisfying than sowing a row of vegetables and then catching that first glimpse of fragile green shoots breaking through the soil a few days later.

Most (but not all) common garden vegetables are grown from seeds. Nurseries and garden centers usually have a good selection of seeds in the spring, but for the best choice of cultivars and varieties, order seeds from one of the many mail-order suppliers. Their catalogs usually start arriving in the mail in early fall, and the earlier you place your order, the more likely you will get your pick of the vegetables you want. Alternatively, many interesting seeds are sold on Internet sites. Don't be tempted by glossy pictures to buy seeds that are unsuitable for your climate.

Above: Young leaves can be difficult to identify, so make sure you label each row of vegetables to help you remember what you planted—and where.

Opposite: An empty seed packet is a quick way to remind you what you have planted in a seed-starting tray or pot.

TIME SAVER

Large, round pelleted seeds are easier to handle and space out when sowing, saving time in thinning seedlings later.

Decoding the packet

Some of the descriptions on seed packets can be confusing. Here are a few terms that describe the type of seeds.

Cultivar: Meaning "cultivated variety," a plant that has been created or selected and maintained by gardeners. Often simply referred to as a "variety," which is a strain of a plant species with the same characteristics, such as leaf shape, size, color, or growth rate. The part of a plant name set inside single quote marks, such as Tomato 'Tom Thumb', identifies the cultivar.

F1 hybrids: Seeds from a deliberate cross between two varieties. They may be expensive but produce uniform crops. Seeds from these plants won't produce the same type of plant, so don't save them.

Open pollinated: Seeds from plants that have been fertilized naturally. They can produce the same, "true" plant as the parent plant if fertilized by the same variety.

Pelleted: Small, oddly shaped seeds covered with an inert claylike material to make them easier to handle.

Treated: These seeds are pretreated with a fungicide to prevent disease. They are dyed to identify them as chemically treated.

Sowing outside

Many vegetables are sown outdoors in the open, directly where they will grow. Direct sowing starts in early to midspring and carries on right through until early fall, depending on the type of vegetable. Always check the seed packet for instructions—you can sow some varieties early in the season, but for others you will need to wait until the soil gets warm.

For seeds to grow well, the soil needs to be broken down into finé, even crumbs. Digging beds in fall will allow winter frost to break down lumps and make the soil easier to work. However, before sowing you will need to turn the soil over once again with a fork, and then use a rake to break up any lumps and to smooth the surface until level. Wait until the soil is reasonably dry and crumbly before you prepare it for sowing, because wet soil won't break down to a fine enough texture.

TIME SAVER

When sowing short rows, it is sometimes easier to make a furrow by laying the handle of the rake on the soil surface and treading on it lightly to make a shallow depression.

Sowing in rows

1. Most vegetables are best sown in straight rows, not because they look neat but to make it easier to control weeds and take care of the plants. To lay out the row, use garden string or a piece of twine pulled taut between two stakes. Then create a shallow furrow along the length of the line with the corner edge of a hoe.

The depth of the furrow will depend on the size of the seeds being sown; aim to cover seeds to about their own depth in soil. In dry conditions, water the bottom of the furrow before sowing, using a gentle dribble of water.

2. In general, avoid overcrowding the seeds because crowded seedlings will not develop well and will involve extra work in thinning them out at an early stage. You can carefully tap larger seeds straight out of the packet—creasing the open edge of the packet to form a funnel shape will make this easier. Or take pinches of seeds and sprinkle them thinly along the furrow.

Seeds in a **trench**

1. You can sow some seeds, such as peas and bush bean seeds, in double rows a few inches apart. Leave wider paths between the furrows to make more room for picking. Use a hoe with a 4–6-inch (10–15cm) blade, and keep the depth of the furrow even so all the seeds emerge at the same time. (This technique can also be used for radishes, scallions, and other vegetables that grow close together—thin them out as they grow.)

2. Large seeds, such as beans or zucchini, are easy to handle, so you can space them individually. However, you should sow a few extra in case some of the seeds fail to germinate, which often happens.

Seed **aftercare**

Fill in the furrow by pulling the soil back evenly with the rake, and tread or tamp it down lightly. Don't forget to label the row with the vegetable sown and the date. If watering is needed before the seeds germinate or while seedlings are small, use a fine spray attachment on the hose or watering can.

Sowing in **clusters**

Some vegetables, such as Swiss chard and kohlrabi, need to be spaced more widely apart. To reduce the amount of seeds you use, sow them in small clusters at intervals along the furrow. (Not all the seeds will germinate, so sow several seeds in each cluster.) If the eventual spacing of plants should be 18 inches (45cm), sow clusters every 9 inches (23cm). First, thin each cluster so only the strongest seedling remains; then once the plants are big enough to use, remove every other one to eat as baby vegetables, leaving the remainder (which will now be at the correct spacing) to grow to full size.

Sowing in containers

There are several reasons why you might want to sow your vegetables in containers instead of directly into the soil where you want them to grow.

Above: Seed-starting kits come with a transparent plastic propagator top, which helps seeds germinate.

Opposite above left: Large seeds are easy to sow into individual compartments.

Opposite above right: Seeds planted in the right conditions will soon emerge as healthy young seedlings.

Opposte bottom right: Having room to grow produces strong, sturdy plants.

Sowing seeds in containers enables you to get an early start. You can sow them indoors—either in a greenhouse or sunroom, or even on a sunny windowsill inside the house—while the weather outside is still too cold, or the soil is too wet. It also makes maximum use of the available space. You can start raising the next batch of plants so that they are ready to replace an existing crop after it is harvested.

Starting seeds in containers can be more economical. Because indoor seedlings are easier to look after, you are more likely to raise the maximum number of healthy plants from expensive seeds. In addition, when a small number of plants is needed, it is often easier to look after them in their early stages if they are sown in containers.

Types of containers

What kind of container you use will depend on the number of plants you want and on how long they will stay indoors before being planted outside. There are two basic types of containers to consider. Seed-starting trays have individual compartments joined together, making it easier for you to water a number of plants at the same time. However, they are shallow, so seedlings run out of room for their roots quickly. For a small number of plants, such as a few tomatoes, sow seeds in 3½-inch (9cm) pots. These are deeper than trays, so the seedlings do not need repotting as quickly. You can attach a plastic propagator top to both trays and pots, which will keep warmth and humidity high to encourage germination.

TIME SAVER

You can sow fast-maturing summer crops for pots and tubs, such as baby leaf salad greens and radishes, directly into the containers in which they will grow until harvesting.

How to sow

Fill the container with a good-quality seed-starting mix. Level the mix and press it down lightly; then water it with a fine nozzle attachment on a watering can. Allow the water to drain before sowing.

Either space individual seeds by hand or scatter them thinly over the surface of the soil mix, and cover them with a layer of soil mix (the seed packet will tell you to what depth they need to be covered). Simply push large seeds beneath the surface of the potting mix to cover them.

Cover the newly sown trays or pots with a plastic propagator top or a sheet of glass; then—except for celery and some types of lettuce, which need more light—lay a sheet of newspaper on top. This covering keeps in both warmth and moisture to create the humid atmosphere seeds need for germination to take place. Put the container in an evenly warm spot, and keep the soil mix just moist.

As soon as the first seedlings start to emerge, remove the newspaper layer and move the container to a position with good lighting, such as near a window. Water the soil mix carefully when the seedlings appear—it is easy to knock them over with a strong jet of water.

Moving on

When seedlings in the container start to become crowded, repot them to give them more space. Do this as soon as the seedlings are large enough to handle easily. You can use a dibble to lift the young plants, handling them only by their seed leaves—the first pair of leaves that appear. Either move the seedlings to another tray, spacing them farther apart, or repot them individually. Sowing seeds thinly in the first place will save you time because you can avoid the need for repotting altogether.

Vegetables for transplanting

Vegetable plants that have been started in containers, or that have been bought from a store, need to be transplanted to the open garden or a larger container where they can mature. Transplanting almost always involves some damage to the roots, which can stunt the plant's growth. Be careful to keep root damage to a minimum, and look after the transplants carefully in their first few days in their new home.

Buying young plants

Raising transplants from seeds is fun and satisfying, but it is not always practical. When you are short of time and need only a small number of plants, it is often easier (and sometimes cheaper) to buy a few young started plants from a nursery or garden center instead of raising your own from seeds. The kind of plants it might make sense to buy include tomatoes, peppers, and zucchini.

However, consider their price, because sometimes the cost per plant is two or three times what you would pay for the same vegetable sold ready to eat in the grocery store. This is especially the case for mail-order plants, when the cost of delivery can provide the final sting that makes the price prohibitive.

When buying plants, look for those that are fresh and healthy, with a strong growing point. Avoid plants that have been in their pots so long that the roots are completely filling the container and thrusting through the drainage holes. These plants are potbound and their

Above: For the best chance of success, choose started vegetable plants that have lush, healthy-looking leaves.

Right: Yellow leaves on a started vegetable plant can indicate that the soil was allowed to dry out or that the plant has been in its pot for so long that the roots have become pot-bound.

growth will have been stunted by the cramped conditions. Buy from a supplier where you can see young plants are well maintained and watered regularly, not left to wilt in the hot sun or dry out in the wind.

Difficult customers

Some plants don't like transplanting and are best sown directly where they will grow. Root crops, such as carrots, are particularly difficult because the slightest damage to the young root will result in a misshapen carrot. Other plants resent the interruption to growth that they almost inevitably receive on transplanting. In response, they can bolt—produce seeds too early—which makes the crop useless. Lettuce, spinach, and Asian greens can be prima donnas in this way. If you want to transplant these crops, choose (or grow) plants sown individually in soil blocks or fiber pots, and plant them in the ground still in the pots to avoid any root disturbance.

Hardening off

Plants that are raised in a greenhouse or under cover, either by yourself or by a supplier, need to gradually get used to outdoor conditions. This is known as hardening off. Ideally, it takes about a week to get plants used to the harsher conditions outdoors. Start by setting them outside in a sheltered spot on a warm day—in the corner of a patio, for example, or against a sunny wall—and putting them back indoors at night. After a few days, leave them outside in their sheltered position at night as well; then move them onto a more open, less-sheltered position for one or two days before planting in the ground.

Left: Plants that are gradually hardened off won't receive the sudden shock that would interrupt their growth; this can occur if they are moved straight from warm conditions to their outdoor planting spot.

Planting transplants

Unlike seeds, when started vegetable plants and transplants are ready to be planted outdoors, you won't need to do much soil preparation. However, transplants will still need just a little attention to make sure they get a good start in their new home.

In sunny weather, move transplants outdoors in the evening ...

Setting out young plants

Choose a still, overcast day for transplanting. Because there is usually root damage in the transplanting process, the young plants often find it difficult to get enough water from the ground to replace that being lost from their leaves. This is why transplants tend to wilt soon after being planted outdoors. Hot, sunny or windy conditions make the wilting worse. In sunny weather, move transplants outdoors in the evening so that they have the relative cool of nighttime to recover.

Always give transplants a thorough soaking a couple of hours before moving them outdoors. If the weather is hot and dry, water the area where they will be planted, too. Do this the day before planting—the water will have time to penetrate deeply into the soil and drain away so that the surface will be workable, not muddy.

Planting from individual pots

Plants growing in individual pots are the least likely to have root damage. For the best

Planting outdoors

1. To remove a plant from a plastic pot, support the plant stem with your index and middle fingers. Turn the pot upside down, and firmly tap the rim of the pot on a firm surface. The root-ball should slide out easily.

2. If the roots are packed tightly, loosen them gently. Set the plant in the hole so that the top of the root-ball is just below the surface. Make sure the bottom of the plant is sitting firmly on the soil at the bottom of the hole.

3. Pull the soil back to fill in the hole, and press it in gently but thoroughly using your fingers and knuckles or the ball of your foot.

Check at what distance your transplants should be spaced and find a handy way to measure it. Knowing your hand span or the length of your thumb, trowel, or foot can make it much quicker to measure the correct spacing between plants.

results, the pots should be filled just with roots so that the root-ball comes out cleanly.

First prepare the planting area: turn over the soil over; remove any weeds and large stones; and rake the soil. Set the planting line—such as a taut string held between two stakes—in place if you are using one, and stand the plants, still in their pots, in their planting positions. Before removing each plant from its pot, dig a planting hole using a trowel, making it both deep and wide enough to fit the roots comfortably.

Fiber pots decompose in the soil, so you don't need to remove the plants from the pots before planting them into the ground. Not only does this speed up the planting process, it also helps to avoid root damage. However, you do need to make sure the pot is well soaked and the soil in the planting bed is thoroughly watered to encourage the roots to grow through the fiber, or they can remain bound inside the pot. You can tear one side of the pot just to make sure this doesn't happen.

Planting from a seed tray

No matter how hard you try, plants that are not raised in individual pots will have some root damage on transplanting. If you leave them in the tray for too long before transplanting, the roots become matted and entangled with one another and are hard to separate. (If this does happen, try to carefully tease them apart with your fingers.)

Water the plants thoroughly several hours before planting them outdoors. To remove the plants from the tray, knock the bottom of the tray on a firm surface, and shake it until the soil mix loosens; then pry up a clump of plants. Plant them as you would plants from individual pots. (See "Planting Outdoors," opposite page.)

Above: Once transplants are in the ground, water the plants thoroughly, and keep them well watered over the next few days if the weather is dry.

Well-contained
vegetables

It's surprising how many vegetables you can grow successfully in containers. You might not get such a high yield from some plants as you would with those planted in the open ground, but that's a small price to pay for being able to grow your own food where open-ground planting is simply not an option. Container-grown vegetables often are ready for harvesting more quickly, too, making them a great choice for time-conscious growers.

Gallon pots

Pots come in many shapes and sizes, so it's often more useful to give their volume. As a guide, a round pot 13 inches (32cm) across and 7½ inches (19cm) high holds 4 gallons (15L); a pot 9 inches (23cm) across and 10 inches (25cm) high holds 2½ gallons (10L).

Planter types

Containers for plants come in all shapes and sizes, and in a wide range of materials. If you have only a small garden that needs to be decorative as well as productive, the appearance of the containers is likely to be just as important as their practical virtues.

Where size is concerned, generally it's a case of the bigger, the better (within reason), although the size will vary according to the plant and variety. You can grow small plants, such as annual herbs and cherry tomatoes, for example, in a 1-gallon (4-L) pot, but 3–4 gallons (12–15L) is a better minimum size for most vegetables. Remember that large pots need a lot of potting mix to fill them—and they will be heavy to move once filled and planted.

Hanging baskets: These are less commonly used for vegetables because they contain such a small volume of potting mix, but they are great for trailing herbs, such as thyme, and cherry tomatoes.

Window boxes: Again, they don't offer much growing space, but compact varieties of carrots, bush

Tubs and pots: Round pots are the most common shape of all. However, you can get a range of different shapes, such as the square Versailles planter or a hexagonal wooden planter. Many planters have a slightly tapered shape so that you can stack them inside each other when not in use—this is a useful feature in a small garden where storage space is in short supply.

Above: Use your imagination to create a personal container—in this case, a kitchen colander has been converted into a home for delicious, sweet strawberries.

Growing in a bag

Turn a bag of potting mix into a planter. Tomatoes and peppers are good choices for bags. Lay the unopened bag flat on the ground where the plants will grow, and use a sharp knife to make three planting holes (cut a cross in the plastic and tuck the flaps in). Or remove the plastic over the top surface of the bag, leaving a few inches around the edge, and sow salad greens or lettuce in the soil.

surface; this prevents water-logging, but the soil in them can dry out more quickly.

Wood: Although wooden containers are attractive, wood rots when wet. A wooden planter can have a short life if not lined and treated. Cheap containers are made of softwood; longer-lasting hardwoods can be more expensive.

beans, tomatoes, herbs, and leafy salad greens will all do well in window boxes. However, you need to make sure you feed and water them frequently.

Material world

The material you choose for your containers depends on personal preference and your budget. These are some of the more common types available in garden centers.

Plastic: Lightweight, so they are easy to carry, but plastic containers might be blown over in windy spots. They do not shatter like clay if dropped, but they are still easily damaged and tend to have a limited life. They retain moisture well and are cheap. Basic plastic pots are not attractive, but there are plenty of convincing terra-cotta-style containers available for a fraction of the price of the real thing.

Clay (terra-cotta): Clay pots look good but have their drawbacks. They are heavy, expensive, easily broken when dropped, and can be damaged by frost. However, they are more stable than plastic. They are porous, so water evaporates from their

Metal: With their sharp, clean lines, these are popular in many modern-style gardens. They are usually made of steel galvanized with zinc. Stainless-steel planters are also available and look stunning, but they are expensive. Be careful when using antique metal containers—some are lined with lead, so they should never be used for growing food.

Above left: When arranging your planters, put smaller ones in front to make sure the plants get enough sun.

Above: A wine bottle cooler has found new life as a container for a chili plant.

Below: The flowers on a zucchini make this an attractive vegetable choice for a container—as pretty as any plant in bloom.

Planting your containers

Because vegetables in containers are growing in a limited quantity of potting mix, they will need a little more care than if they were growing in the open ground. However, if you start them off right, you will save yourself a lot of time and trouble.

TIME SAVER

Hanging baskets are so packed with plants and roots that water tends to run straight off the surface of the potting mix, making watering messy and time consuming. When planting the basket, sink a small plastic flowerpot in the soil mix so that its top is level with the surface. Pour into this pot when watering—it will act as a reservoir and make watering the basket much easier.

Vegetables suitable for containers

Baby beets
Blueberries
Carrots (short-
    root varieties)
Bush and pole
    beans
Herbs
Kohlrabi
Lettuce
Peppers and
    chilies
Potatoes
Radishes
Salad greens
Strawberries
Tomatoes

Above right : Vegetables and herbs can be partnered in container planters, such as this upright pepper plant and trailing thyme.

Water and drainage

Vegetables growing in containers are often exposed to both drought and waterlogging because there is a limited amount of potting soil around the roots, which can cause problems. Roots need air as well as water, so while there should always be enough water in the soil for a plant's needs, excess water must also be able to drain away freely. The smaller the container, the more difficult it is to get this juggling act just right.

When you choose a container, make sure that it has enough drainage holes. If you decide to transform another object into a container, you may need to make drainage holes—make sure you select a container in a material into which you will be able to make holes. (This could involve drilling, so choose wisely.)

Before planting the container, you will also need to make sure that the drainage holes will not get blocked. For example, you can use a layer of clay pieces from a broken terra-cotta pot or stones at the bottom of the pot—in other words, large material that water can easily trickle under. Raise the container off the ground on pot feet, blocks of wood, or bricks so that water can easily drain.

The ABCs of container soil

The next step is to choose a soil mix that will not dry out too quickly. You can use regular soil from your yard, but you may transfer diseases along with it. Instead, use a good-quality potting mix, which will be free of pests and diseases. Soil-based potting mixes have long-lasting supplies of nutrients and retain water best, but they are heavy, making the bags and filled pots awkward to move. Soilless growing media are based on peat or a peat alternative, such as coir or bark. They are lightweight and clean to handle, but they dry out quickly and need frequent watering and feeding. They can be difficult to rewet if they dry out, but good brands have a wetting agent to help dry media reabsorb water quickly.

You can mix water-retaining granules with the potting mix as you fill the container. These granules soak up water like a sponge and hold it for plants to use without the soil mix becoming waterlogged. The downside is that they can be damaging to soil life.

A supporting role

Some plants, such as tomatoes or beans, will need some type of support as they mature. Put these in place early, before the plant has time to grow too much, to avoid root damage and to give the plants support as soon as they need it.

Container aftercare

Keep a careful eye on the moisture level of the potting mix, especially on hot or windy days. Most containers need daily watering, and hanging baskets may even need watering twice a day. Aim to keep the potting mix slightly moist at all times.

After you plant the vegetables, you can cover the surface of the soil mix with a mulch—a layer of gravel, pebbles, or shredded bark, for example. Not only will it help prevent water from evaporating, thereby cutting down on the amount of water needed, it will also look more attractive.

Container-grown plants will also need feeding. Liquid food is most quickly absorbed; use high-nitrogen fertilizer for leafy growth and high potassium for fruits and flowers (that

includes vegetables such as beans, broccoli, zucchini, peas, and tomatoes, as well as blueberries and strawberries). Different fertilizer brands are applied at different rates and varying intervals, so follow the package directions. (See "Food for Thought," pages 54–55.)

Big pots

If you use a large container, make sure you place it in its final position BEFORE you start filling it with potting mix. A large pot filled with soil will be heavy and difficult to move. Special pot caddies with wheels are designed to help make heavy plant containers more portable.

Planting containers

1. Fill the container halfway to two-thirds with potting mix. Carefully support the plant's stem as you remove the plant from the plastic pot by giving the rim of the pot a firm tap; gently loosen the roots a bit if necessary.

2. Pull back the potting mix to make room for the plant's roots. If the container will hold only one plant, put it in the center; otherwise, check the position of all the plants before you plant the first one.

3. Once all the plants are in position, fill in around them with more potting mix; then press them in gently but thoroughly. Finally, water them thoroughly to help them get settled.

Watering

Roots: A plant's life support

Plants get their water supply from the soil, where it is held in pockets between soil particles. Branching roots spread throughout the soil as tiny root hairs suck up moisture, which is taken up through the stem and transported to all parts of the plant. Because moisture evaporates from the surface of the leaves, plants need a continual supply of fresh water at the roots to replace it.

If a plant does not get enough moisture, eventually the cells become limp and the plant wilts—an obvious sign that it is desperate for water. However, damage can be done even before this stage is reached.

There are two main reasons why a plant is not getting enough water: either there is no water available in the soil, or the roots and their delicate hairs have been damaged so that they cannot supply enough water for the plant's needs. Roots can be damaged by overenthusiastic firming during planting, by careless soil cultivation near the plant, by soil-living pests, such as grubs and maggots, and by drought or (paradoxically) waterlogging.

Fixing the soil

If there is no water in the soil, this is usually because it has not rained, but it can also be because the soil drains too freely. You can improve fast-draining sandy soil by adding organic matter, such as well-rotted garden compost or manure; the texture of organic matter will soak up and hold the moisture.

A mulch slows down evaporation from the soil, so apply a layer of garden compost or a store-bought mulching product, or cover the soil surface with black plastic sheets available from garden centers. Be sure the soil is thoroughly moist before you do so.

Don't forget that weeds also steal water from your vegetables, which is a good reason to keep them under control. (see "Weeding Out the Competition," pages 60–61.)

All plants need water in order to survive, but sometimes a little extra at the right time can make the difference between a reasonable harvest and a truly bumper crop. Natural rainfall is not always enough to keep plants thriving—especially in small gardens, where surrounding walls and buildings, overhanging trees and shrubs, and paved surfaces can make it difficult for rain to penetrate to where it is needed. However, watering at the wrong time can often be a waste of both water and your efforts.

When to water

Whether or not you will need to water obviously depends on the weather—if your summer is blighted by torrential rain, at least you won't need to get out the hose. However, there are certain conditions when it is important to water all plants.

In weather that is dry, when plants are at risk of wilting, particularly if it is also hot or windy, you need to water plants because they will lose even more moisture from their leaves. Don't judge if a plant needs watering by the surface of the soil. Using a trowel, dig a hole near the plant serveral inches deep so that you can see how dry the soil is in the root zone.

Plants need watering immediately after transplanting, and for several days afterward, until they are settled. Watering is also necessary after thinning out seedlings because the roots of the remaining plants will have been disturbed as a nearby plant is pulled out. Otherwise, provide water only when plants will get the most benefit, as below.

Fruit-bearing plants: Blueberries, strawberries, beans, peas, peppers and chilies, zucchini and squash, tomatoes. Watering at the right time is crucial for this group because watering too soon will encourage leafy growth at the expense of flowers and the fruit and seeds that follow. Wait until the first flowers appear; then keep the soil thoroughly moist all the time while the crop is developing. This can greatly improve the overall harvest.

Root vegetables: Beet, carrots, potatoes, radish, turnips, and kohlrabi (which is not really a root but is treated like one here). A sudden increase in water supply often leads to split roots, so keep the soil moisture steady all the time the plants are growing. Be particularly careful to provide enough moisture once the roots have started swelling. Potatoes respond best to watering when the tubers are about the size of marbles, which is after flowering has started.

Leafy vegetables: Arugula, broccoli, Asian greens, celery, mâche, cress, kale, leeks, lettuce, mustard, onions, pea shoots, spinach, and Swiss chard. These plants like plenty of water throughout their life. However, if water (or time) is in short supply, be sure to water plants about 10 days before you expect to harvest the plant. Do not give a sudden deluge of water, as too much all at once can cause maturing lettuce and head-forming greens to split.

Ways to water

Watering vegetables and other plants can be a time-consuming business—especially if you are growing a lot of them in containers—but there are ways to make it quicker and easier.

TIME SAVER

To attach spray guns to the hose or link lengths of hose together, use brass or plastic "push-and-click" connectors. These are much quicker and simpler to use than screw-together fittings.

Lay the [soaker] hose ... so that the water goes exactly where it is needed, near the roots—and little, if any, is lost by evaporation.

Watering methods

What method of watering you use will depend on the size of your garden—and also your budget. Several options are listed below.

Watering can: The cheap, simple method for small gardens. Choose a well-balanced can that is easy to carry. Don't be tempted to go for one that is too large—full cans of water are heavy, especially after making several trips back and forth to the faucet. A long spout makes reaching distant plants easier. Buy a "rose" to fit the spout—this attachment breaks up the water into fine droplets that will not damage plants or wash seedlings out of the soil.

Hose: A hose is a much quicker, easier way to water your garden than a watering can. It is a good idea to keep the hose neatly stowed on a reel, especially in a small garden where space is at a premium. Use a spray-nozzle attachment on the end of the hose to break up the water into droplets.

Soaker hose: Lengths of this type of hose are perforated or made from porous material to let water gently seep out of the hose along its length. Lay the hose along the rows of plants so that the water goes to exactly where it is needed, near the roots—and little, if any, is lost by evaporation. A soaker hose is a good time saver, too. You can simply turn on the water and leave it unattended for several hours to soak the soil. Placing the hose near the plants' roots helps keep the soil between the rows from getting wet, which discourages weed growth—yet another time-saving benefit.

Automatic watering system: This is the most labor- and time-saving way to water your plants, but it is also the most expensive. It involves connecting a main supply hose to a faucet with a pressure regulator; then connecting lengths of micro hoses leading off the main hose to deliver water to the plants via drippers, sprinklers, or soaker hoses. You can open and close the valve as required or automate the whole process by using a timer. If you are eager to conserve water, you can link an automatic timer to a rain sensor, which will cancel a timed watering program when a certain amount of rain is detected.

Conserving water

It makes sense to ensure that the natural water supply goes as far as possible. This not only will save you time spent watering but will help to conserve what is often a limited resource—particularly important in dry regions and if you are paying for a metered water supply. Add as much bulky organic matter to the soil as possible, whether it is garden compost, farmyard manure, leaf mold, or store-bought bags of soil amendments. In spring, when the soil is most likely to be thoroughly moist, apply a good layer of mulch over the soil surface to help prevent evaporation.

Opposite: A watering can is ideal when you have only a few plants or containers to water, but for a larger garden, invest in some type of hose or automatic watering system.

Food for thought

Plants manufacture their own food from sunlight. However, to keep that process in action, they need some other supplies, which they generally get from the soil. If you have a rich, fertile soil, the necessary nutrients will be present in abundance; yet often the soil is not that good and you will need to supplement the food supply by adding fertilizers.

The big three

The three main nutrients a plant needs are nitrogen, phosphorus, and potassium. These are often referred to by their chemical symbols, N, P, and K. Each nutrient has a complex role within the plant, but in a simplified form, nitrogen promotes leafy growth, phosphorus ensures healthy roots and shoots, and potassium encourages the formation of flowers and fruit, as well as plant hardiness.

Minor nutrients

Other chemicals are needed by plants, including manganese, iron, sulfur, calcium, and magnesium. Sufficient amounts are usually present in most soil because only tiny quantities are needed by plants. However, deficiencies do occur and can cause striking symptoms. Leaves with distinct yellow margins or bright green veins standing out against a yellow background signal that some of these minor nutrients are in short supply. Look for a fertilizer, such as a foliar fertilizer, with "trace elements" to rectify the problem.

A balancing act

Different brands of fertilizers contain varying quantities and proportions of plant foods. You can quickly see what type of food a brand provides by checking the package. The ratios of nitrogen, phosphorus, and potassium are printed as NPK levels (always in that order). For example, a package labeled NPK 7-7-7 is a balanced fertilizer containing all the major nutrients in equal proportions; 5-5-10 contains all three nutrients but has a higher proportion of potassium (K), and 21-0-0 has only nitrogen (N).

A high-nitrogen fertilizer is suitable for leafy vegetables, such as spinach, while a high-potassium fertilizer is good for fruiting-type crops, such as tomatoes. Balanced fertilizers are a good general insurance policy for most vegetables. Apply a balanced fertilizer routinely when preparing the soil for sowing and planting in spring. After that, apply fertilizers as needed through the growing season, following the detailed instructions on the packaging.

Types of fertilizers

There are different ways to apply fertilizers—the choice you make usually depends on the reason for using them.

Liquids: Fertilizers in liquid form are usually quickly absorbed by plants. Liquid fertilizers are almost always concentrated and need to be diluted with water before application. Check the directions on the label.

Powders: You need to apply powdered fertilizer either straight from the package to the soil or dissolved in water before application; check the instructions carefully. Dry powdered fertilizers can scorch the young leaves and growing tips of plants, so apply them carefully on a still day. Don't spread them right up against plant stems. Lightly rake the fertilizer into the soil surface after application.

Granules: Granular fertilizers are usually spread on the soil surface. They are easier to handle and, therefore, quicker to apply than powders. They are also less likely to scorch plants or to be blown around by the wind.

Foliar fertilizers: Plants can absorb nutrients through their leaves as well as their roots, and foliar fertilizers produce a rapid response. Choose a specially formulated foliar fertilizer because normal fertilizers are not suitable.

Opposite: Lush, healthy leaves are a good sign that these plants have plenty of the right nutrients, especially nitrogen.

Supporting roles

There are several reasons why gardeners provide support for some vegetable plants. Support systems enable them to make the maximum use of space and keep the vegetables off the soil. They also make the vegetables more convenient and quicker to harvest, saving both time and irritation.

Crops that need support

Climbing beans (depending on the variety)
Bush beans (depending on the variety)
Chilies
Peas
Tomatoes

Providing supports will let the plants grow by extending upward instead of rambling over the ground, which is especially important in small gardens. In addition, keeping the vegetables off the soil will help keep them protected from attack by pests, such as slugs, and diseases that thrive in the damp conditions.

Fortunately, the majority of fast-growing vegetables don't need support from gardeners. They are either low growing or are harvested so quickly that they don't need a support system. Check the descriptions of cultivars and varieties in a seed catalog. Many are bred to be especially compact, so some varieties are much less likely to need staking than others.

However, there are vegetable varieties that will produce much better results with a helping hand. Always get supports in early, before they are needed, which will help to prevent root damage. There are several types of supports.

Right: Cages come in all kinds of three-dimensional forms, including square, triangular, circular, and tapering spiral shapes.

Above right: Use garden string, plastic plant ties, or even strips of cloth to gently tie a plant to a supporting stake.

Cages: Good for tomatoes and peppers, plant cages are three-dimensional supports in which the plant is set in the center and grows up through the structure. They save time because plants growing in them need less tying than when grown with other types of supports.

Individual stakes: Vegetables such as tomatoes and chilies are reasonably stocky. However, as they grow and, hopefully, carry a heavy crop, they tend to lean, sometimes down to the ground. At planting time, provide each plant with a sturdy stake set about 1 foot (30cm) deep; then tie the main stem to it at intervals as the plant grows taller. Make sure the tie isn't so tight that it will cut into the stem as the plant grows.

Groups of stakes: In small gardens, support climbing beans on tepees of tall stakes or poles arranged in a circle and tied or clipped together at the top. This method saves space and looks attractive, too. You can also arrange the stakes in a double row in an A-frame shape, with pairs of stakes tied together and more stakes laid horizontally to form a ridge and tied firmly into place to keep the structure secure. You can attach horizontal string or guy wires to the end stakes to provide supports for the plants.

Netting: Wide mesh netting, supported on sturdy stakes, will soon be covered by the scrambling growth of peas or beans. However, be careful: unless it is firmly

Trellis: A wooden trellis secured to a wall or fence is useful for climbing beans to scramble through. You can use a freestanding trellis to support spreading zucchini and squash plants, making them an attractive feature. (Check whether your particular squash is a sprawling vine variety or a more compact bush type.)

Branched brush: Supports made of winter prunings taken from live hardwood shrubs are perfect for plants that have twining tendrils, such as peas. They will also help to hold up bushy plants, such as bush beans. Use branches with plenty of twigs about 3 feet (1m) tall. Push them into the soil about 1 foot (30cm) apart along the row as soon as you see seedlings emerging.

secured, the weight of the plant can pull it down or cause it to fall as the season progresses. Disentangling dead plant growth at the end of the season can be a frustrating job. This often means that the netting gets only one season of use before being disposed of, making it an expensive option.

Top: Tepees not only provide support but also help to save space in a small garden.

Above: Branched brush will keep plants upright and the crop off the ground.

Going under cover

A little extra protection for the soil and your plants can help your crops reach harvest time more quickly. There are several easy ways to protect vegetables from the extremes of Mother Nature.

Make a quick and easy temporary cloche to cover a young plant by cutting off the bottom of a large, plastic beverage bottle. Place the top of the bottle directly over the plant, and remove the screw cap for ventilation during the day. This is a great method for protecting tender plants, such as tomatoes and chilies, when they are first planted outdoors.

... the main warming effect comes from keeping the rain off the soil.

Protecting the soil

In early spring, sowing and planting can be held up because the soil conditions are not right, even if the weather itself is fine. While a light, crumbly textured soil warms up early, enabling you to get going as soon as the weather allows, heavy clay soil takes a long time to warm up and dry out. The first step is to improve drainage and soil texture by working in organic matter. (See

"Ground Rules," pages 32–33.) However, placing a cover over your sowing and planting area will also help the soil to warm quickly. You can use glass cloches, which act like mini greenhouses to trap the sun's heat, but their main warming effect comes from keeping the rain off the soil. Using a sheet of black plastic will also absorb the sun's heat, warming the soil and keeping it dry.

Protecting the plants

Once you sow your seeds or plant young plants in the ground, you can encourage them to grow more quickly by giving them protection from the weather. You will need to take your garden conditions into account when deciding whether it's worth giving plants extra protection. In a sheltered, warm and sunny yard, they will grow well without additional help. However, if they are in an open spot exposed to cold winds in a chilly spring, it's a different matter.

Protection is often necessary only when the plants are getting established early in the season. However, at the other end of the year, it will help to keep tender plants, such as tomatoes, producing a crop longer into the cooler fall days.

Forms of protection

There are several different ways of providing that little extra help for your plants.

Cloches and tunnels:
Cloches, which are also sometimes called "hot caps," are plant covers originally made from glass, but today plastic is more popular. While plastic is not as efficient at trapping heat, it is lighter and easier to move than glass, and much less fragile. Cloches may be semicircular or an A-frame or barn shape. They are usually about 2 feet (60cm) long so that they can be moved from plant to plant or placed end to end to form a continuous row.

Tunnels consist of wire hoops set over the row of plants to be protected, covered with a thin polyethylene plastic sheet. Sometimes sheets of other materials are used. On hot days, roll back the sheet to prevent the plants from becoming overheated.

Floating row covers:
There are different types available. They protect plants from both weather and pest attack. Some are so light that you can lay them directly over the plants without damaging them. These are made of a lightweight material of woven plastic fabric. Although this looks insubstantial, it can make a surprising difference to plant growth.

Weigh down the corners and edges with stones, or dig them into the soil, to keep the cover from blowing away. Alternatively, stretch them over hoops to form tunnels, or make frames to support them over beds. You can also use a floating row cover over soil in early spring to help it warm up quickly. However, because it lets rain through, it is not as effective as a solid barrier, such as black plastic sheets.

Raised bed protection

You can buy raised bed kits complete with covers, providing you with a metal frame that fits neatly over the bed and a fine mesh cover to slip over the frame. The sides of the mesh cover can be opened for access, and there is plenty of headroom for the crops, which will be protected from both adverse weather and pests.

Opposite: Plastic cloches come in many shapes and forms, such as this semicircular example with ventilation openings. You can remove them during the daytime to let plenty of fresh air reach young plants, replacing them at night to provide protection from the cold.

Above: Even when crops are almost ready for harvesting, a floating row cover will be beneficial because it acts as a barrier to pests.

Weeding out the competition

Weeds are bad news. They make your garden look untidy, and more importantly, they compete with your plants for light, space, food, and water. They can also harbor pests and diseases that will attack your vegetables.

TIME SAVER

While hot, dry weather is best for hoeing so that severed weed tops shrivel and die quickly, hand weeding is quicker and easier when the soil is moist.

Weeds are everywhere. Hundreds of weed seeds already lie dormant deep in the soil, gradually working their way up nearer the soil surface where they can germinate. Seeds float in on the breeze from adjoining yards, or they hitch a ride on the dirt that clings to the soles of your shoes. Fresh weed seeds and seedlings arrive with every new plant you bring into your plot. You can't avoid them—but you can keep them under control.

Dealing with weeds should not be back-breaking or time-consuming work. It's only when you let them get out of control that they become a real problem. Do what you can to prevent weeds from occurring in the first place; then take a few moments each day to deal with invaders as soon as they raise their heads above ground. Little and often is the key to keeping weeds at bay.

Prevention is better than the cure

Keep down the number of weeds by following these basic rules.

Start clear: When preparing the ground for a new vegetable plot, try to remove all the roots and stems of perennial weeds that you come across. Let freshly dug soil lie empty for a couple of weeks. A flush of weeds will crop up from seeds that have been brought near the surface with the digging. Use a hoe to remove them before you start sowing and planting.

Don't let weeds flower: "One year's seeding, seven years' weeding," as the saying goes. Remove weeds before they have a chance to flower, and you will prevent hundreds more weed seeds

from being sprinkled over your soil to plague you in the years to come.

Cover up:
Bare soil is an open invitation to weeds. Use a mulch to cover the soil surface. There are plenty of packaged products available based on materials such as shredded bark and cocoa hulls, or you can use well-rotted compost from your compost pile, if you have one.

Black plastic:
Spread sheets of black plastic over a whole area before planting. Although not particularly attractive, the plastic is perfect for preventing weed growth.

Target food and water:
Apply water and fertilizers directly to the plants for which they are intended, instead of spreading them over a larger area where weeds can benefit from them, too. A soaker hose is ideal for precision watering of rows of vegetables. (See "Ways to Water," page 53.) Apply plant foods in a narrow band alongside the plant row instead of spreading them over the whole bed.

Dealing with the enemy
Keep a well-sharpened hoe on hand near your vegetables, and deal with weed seedlings as soon as they appear. Don't try to dig them up—slide the hoe along the ground to slice off the top growth. Where weeds are growing right up against plants, weed by hand carefully to avoid accidents with the hoe.

Hand weeding is not an arduous job if it is done often, while the weeds are tiny. In a small garden, it should only take a few minutes each day. While a few weeds will pop up in mulching material, such as compost or bark, the loose nature of the material makes it easy to pull them.

Chemical weed killers are rarely necessary in a small garden, but products such as glyphosate can be useful in clearing a truly weed-infested plot when starting from scratch. There are several weed-killing products based on natural ingredients, such as citrus oils and fatty acids. However, if it will kill weeds, it will kill your vegetable plants, too, so you need to be careful when applying herbicide sprays.

Opposite: When weeds appear too close to plants for hoeing, hand weeding is the best method for removing them.

Above left: Use a sharp knife to cut X-shaped slits through black plastic to create planting holes.

Below: The long handle on a hoe lets you remove the weeds without having to bend down, taking the strain off your back.

A plan for the troublemakers

Gardeners are not the only ones eagerly looking forward to enjoying vegetable and fruit crops—there's a whole army of garden pests waiting to get their teeth into them, too. If the pests don't get them, there's also a range of plant diseases lurking in the wings, ready to wreak havoc.

Exactly what problem strikes your plants depends on where you live and what kind of season it is. Some years can be almost trouble free, while in others, a gardener can face an onslaught of problems, one right after another. Fortunately, there is plenty you can do to turn the scales in your favor.

Preparing for battle

The first step to giving your plants a fighting chance is to grow them in the best possible conditions so that they are strong and vigorous. It won't make them any less attractive to pests and diseases, but it will give them the best opportunity to fight off the ill effects. Avoid putting the plants under any form of stress because this will make them less able to withstand pest and disease attacks.

Choose vegetables that suit your soil and climate, and provide them with a reasonably sheltered, warm position in fertile, fine-textured soil. When you plant them, space them correctly so that there's plenty of air for ventilation. Keep weeds under control so there is no unnecessary competition. Fertilize the vegetables as needed; however, don't overfeed—soft, lush growth is more vulnerable to pest and disease attack. Keep plants watered during dry spells to avoid moisture stress, but don't water foliage excessively, especially in the evening. Damp, cool conditions increase the spread of fungal diseases. Water the

Hairy deer deterrent

Unless you erect an 8-foot-tall (2.5m) fence, it can be difficult to keep deer away from tempting vegetables. One solution worth trying is hanging balls made of human hair wrapped in cheesecloth around the plot to scare them away.

TIME SAVER

Breeders have developed cultivars that are resistant to, or tolerant of, various pests and diseases. For example, tomato 'Legend' has excellent blight tolerance; spinach 'El Grinta' has high resistance to downy mildew; and carrot 'Flyaway' is resistant to carrot-root maggots. Growing resistant cultivars will cut down time spent on checking for and treating problems.

plants overhead in the mornings so that excess moisture has time to evaporate during the sunny part of the day.

Perfect timing

Some vegetable plants have a peak season in which they are attacked by pests. By sowing them early or late, you can avoid their maturing just at the time they are most likely to be attacked. For example, turnips are often attacked by flea beetles, a pest that creates tiny holes in the leaves. If you live in Zones 3–7, try sowing seeds in midsummer instead of spring to early summer, so the plants miss the worst season for attacks. Similarly, if Colorado potato beetles are a problem, plant potato tubers in early summer instead of spring. When the adult beetles emerge from the soil and find no potatoes on your land, they will go elsewhere.

Man the barricades

Many pests can be kept at bay by using physical barriers, and this is particularly appropriate in small gardens. It's much more practical to erect an insect-proof screen over a smallish raised bed than to try to protect an entire large vegetable patch. Fast-growing crops will also need protecting for a relatively short time; a protective structure does not have to be as sturdy and solidly built as if it had to stay in place for a long season.

Glass or plastic cloches or tunnels are handy because they are easy to move from one row of plants to another. (See "Going Under Cover," pages 58–59.) Floating row covers and fine-mesh netting are ideal for keeping out insects.

To keep out large pests, such as birds and four-legged furry mammals, consider a "cage" made of stakes forming a boxlike frame with a covering of a small-mesh netting. To deter rabbits, bury the bottom edges at least 1 foot (30cm) underground, forming the edge into an outward-facing U shape.

It's a cutthroat world

Homemade collars of cardboard or plastic will provide barriers against cutworms. These larvae live about 1 inch (2.5cm) deep in the soil and can demolish seedlings as you sleep at night. For small plants, make a tubelike collar using a toilet tissue or paper towel roll. Cut the top and bottom of a plastic beverage bottle for larger plants. Sink the collar around the plant at planting time so that it's at least 2 inches (5cm) into the ground.

Opposite: Lightweight floating row covers are ideal for keeping flying pests away from carrots. They are so light that you won't need a frame to support them.

Above: Tunnels supporting a netting material will keep birds and smaller pests at bay. Make sure the ends are firmly secured to keep out these critters.

Fighting off the **enemy**

Once pests or diseases attack a plant, it's important to treat the problem promptly before they do too much damage. This means you need to check your plants frequently—and be ready to go on the offense quickly.

Get into the practice of inspecting your vegetables regularly. Look at the undersides of leaves—where trouble often starts—as well as the tops. It can rapidly build up to damaging levels if undetected. You will soon develop an eye for singling out a plant that does not seem quite right and needs additional investigation.

Pest control

Most gardeners prefer to enjoy produce that they know is chemical free. Manufacturers of pesticides have increasingly concentrated on producing short-lived safe products, often made from naturally occurring ingredients.

All garden chemicals are thoroughly tested to ensure they are perfectly safe to use as directed. However, there are other methods you can use on your plants before reaching for a chemical application.

Handpicking: For larger insect pests, such as caterpillars and beetles, you can pick them off plants and drop them into a bowl of soapy water. (If you are squeamish about handling insects, wear gloves.) Where individual picking is not practical, spread a cloth on the ground and shake pest-infested stems over it to dislodge unwelcome visitors. You can use a strong jet of water to dislodge smaller, more tenacious pests, such as clustering aphids—a much quicker option than handpicking.

Trapping: Sink a trap in the ground to capture slugs and snails. Bury an old margarine container with the rim just above soil level (to make it less likely to catch ground beetles, which are garden helpers). Fill the container with diluted beer to attract the slimy critters. They will crawl in—and drown.

Biological controls: Naturally occurring organisms are the biological controls that prey on pest species. Several different types of controls are available from specialty suppliers. (Look for these on the Internet.) Ladybugs and lacewings will attack aphids and other insect pests; nematodes attack slugs and snails; and bacteria attack caterpillars. These all have some success, but biological controls will keep infestations down to acceptable levels instead of wiping them out completely.

Common pests

Below are some of the more common pests that attack vegetable plants and methods for controlling them.

Beetles and bugs (flea beetle, Colorado beetle, striped cucumber beetle, Japanese beetle, Mexican bean bug, tarnished plant bug, squash bug)
Control: Handpick; use insecticides containing soft soap or fatty acids.

Aphids (blackfly and greenfly)
Control: Pick off infested shoot tips; knock pests off with a strong jet of water; use insecticides containing soft soap or fatty acids.

Carrot rust fly
Control: Parasitic nematodes; use floating row covers as a deterrent.

Caterpillars (loopers, cabbage moth caterpillars, tomato hornworm)
Control: Handpick; use biological controls, such as *Bacillus thuringiensis* (Bt), and parasitic nematodes.

Slugs and snails
Control: Handpick; use traps or iron phosphate bait; introduce nematodes.

Plant diseases

Prevention is always better than cure when it comes to diseases. Many are caused by fungi, which thrive in humid, still conditions, so avoid overcrowding plants—they need a good flow of air around them—and don't overwater.

Diseases can also be caused by viruses, which are difficult to control. Distorted growth and yellow streaks or flecks on leaves are indications of a virus attack.

Common diseases

Some of the more common vegetable plant diseases are listed below, along with control methods.

Blossom end rot (tomatoes/peppers)
Control: Never let plants run short of water; add a handful of lime to the watering can.

Botrytis
Control: Remove and destroy affected parts, plus all dead plant debris.

Damping off (seedlings)
Control: Increase the ventilation around seedlings; avoid overcrowding.

Potato blight (potatoes/tomatoes)
Control: Remove affected growth and harvest the potatoes before the disease spreads to tubers in the soil; fungicides may help if applied early.

Mildew (many vegetables)
Control: Improve air flow around plants; pick off affected leaves.

Virus (especially tomatoes/squash)
Control: Remove and burn affected plants; control aphids, which spread virus diseases.

You will soon develop an eye for singling out a plant that does not seem quite right …

Using pesticides safely

Spraying vegetable plants is generally much quicker than picking pests off them by hand, so when time is at a premium you might easily be tempted to turn to garden chemicals. If so, first identify your problem so that you can choose the most appropriate control; then select one that lets you pick and eat treated crops within the shortest possible time. If you want to use organic materials, choose a product with an official organic seal, such as that of the National Organic Program (NOP) or Organic Materials Review Institute (OMRI). Always follow package directions exactly.

Harvest time

It's that moment that rewards all your hard work—the moment when you proudly carry your first crops of the season to the kitchen. With fast-maturing vegetables, you won't have to wait too long for that moment to arrive. You don't always have to wait until a crop is mature.

Pick when large enough

The quickest crops to harvest are sprouting seeds. Just a few days after they have started to grow, they will be ready to eat. When they have grown enough to provide a meal, it will just be a case of giving them a quick rinse before eating.

You can also harvest baby leaf greens as soon as they are large enough to make picking them worthwhile. You can either pick a few leaves at a time from each of several plants of different varieties or cut a number of plants all at once. Leave a stump about 1–2 inches (2.5–5cm) high, and it will resprout to provide another harvest after a couple of weeks. You might even get three or more cuttings from the same plant.

Right: You can usually tell when berries, such as blueberries, are ripe by the color. The deeper the color, the sweeter the berry.

Below: Some vegetables, such as squash, continue to grow quickly once they are ready to harvest. Make sure you inspect and harvest plants regularly before they mature too much.

Opposite: A pair of sharp scissors is ideal for cutting baby leaf greens quickly.

Many plants provide the tastiest, most tender crops if they are picked while young. Marble-size new potatoes have a wonderful flavor, and nothing is sweeter than a tiny baby carrot. However, the total weight of your harvest will be higher if you let the plants grow until they are more bulky. You may prefer to let them grow just a little larger to get a better return for the amount of space the plants have taken up—and for the effort you have put in. A good way to grow many vegetables is to thin the plants out in stages as they grow, eating the thinnings as baby vegetables but leaving suitably spaced plants to grow larger until they are mature.

Pick when they are ripe

Some vegetables need to be left until they are fully developed to be worth eating. Tomatoes, for example, have the best flavor when the fruit is left on the plants until they are completely ripe. If they are picked while still slightly green, they will eventually ripen even off the plant. However, they do not taste as sweet as those that ripen on the vine. You should also let blueberries and strawberries ripen before picking them.

Pick in between

Several crops need to develop to a midway stage, but you can harvest them before they reach full maturity. Peas, for example, need time to flower and develop pods, but you can pick the pods well before the peas inside are mature. Harvest them when the pods are plump, smooth, and green, with the peas inside visible when the pod is held up to the light. The peas should be still small enough to be separate, not touching, in the pod. If the pods are left on the plants until they become dry and parchmentlike, with the peas crammed tightly together inside, they will be mealy and starchy instead of tender and sweet.

Pick beans while they are still young enough to snap crisply in half. Zucchini and summer squash are best harvested while the flower is still attached to the vegetable.

Harvest peppers and chilies at several stages. You can enjoy the immature, green vegetable as soon as it is large enough, but if you leave it on the plant, it will change in color and flavor as it approaches ripeness, becoming sweeter (peppers) or hotter (chilies).

TIME SAVER

Sugar snap peas are eaten complete with their pods, so growing these instead of standard garden peas will save you hours spent shucking peas. The pods are thick and succulent with fully developed peas inside, so you will also get a greater total weight of crop from the same growing area than you would with snow peas that have thin pods.

Harvest basics

Making sure you pick your crops in the right way will enable you to enjoy them at their best. Using the correct harvest techniques can also help to ensure that the plants keep cropping as long as possible.

Above: Picking pea pods before the seeds mature will ensure that new flowers—and a new crop—will keep developing.

Choose the right time of day

The best time to pick most crops is early in the morning, when they contain the most moisture. On hot, sunny days, some crops, such as lettuce and zucchini, can become limp and flabby by the late afternoon or early evening, and they will not be as tasty, or keep as well, if they are picked then.

Cutting

A sharp knife is valuable for harvesting many crops. If you pull up a lettuce by hand, you will often bring up the root as well. Not only will this disturb the roots of the neighboring plants in the row, but it will shower their heads with soil. It's much better to slice the lettuce off cleanly at the base with a knife. Use a sharp knife for picking other leafy crops, such as spinach, too, because pulling leaves away by hand can often loosen the plants in the soil. For baby leaves, a pair of sharp kitchen scissors does the job well.

Plucking

Handle ripe "fruits," such as tomatoes, gently so that you don't bruise them, cupping them in the palm of your hand instead of pinching them with your fingers. Break the stem of tomatoes at the swollen knuckle on the stem so that the spiderlike calyx remains attached to the fruit. You should also pick strawberries complete with the frilly calyx. These fruits will usually keep better if the calyx is still attached.

Pull peas and beans from the plants as they are ready, but be careful that you don't tug too hard and pull the whole plant up by the root, especially in light soil. Hold onto the plant stem with one hand while you pick the pods with the other.

Digging

Lift root crops, such as potatoes, carrots, and beets, and rootlike stems, such as onions and kohlrabi, from the soil. In light, loose soil that contains plenty of organic matter, you can simply pull these vegetables up by hand, but more often it is advisable to use a garden fork—either a hand fork or a full-size border fork, depending on the crop. Drive the fork into the soil a few inches away from the row and lever up the roots carefully. When digging potatoes, remember that the tubers spread widely. If you dig too close to the plant stem, you will probably bring up the fork and find a potato impaled on every prong.

Keep them cropping

A plant's purpose is usually to grow, flower, and produce ripe seeds to perpetuate itself.

The best time to pick most crops is early in the morning, when they contain the most moisture.

Once it has achieved that, its job is done and it will stop cropping. If you want to keep vegetables such as peas, beans, and zucchini producing food for a long period, do not let their seeds mature. This will force the plant into producing more and more seeds to try to achieve its aim. Always pick these kinds of vegetables as soon as they are ready for eating, so they never get a chance to mature fully.

Below: Using a large border fork will enable you to harvest several potatoes at a time— but be careful that you don't spear them.

Save it for later

Whether you simply have too many of one type of vegetable to eat at once, or whether you want to store some so that you can enjoy them at a later date, you need to know the best ways to keep your produce in prime condition.

Crops suitable for freezing

Beans
Broccoli
Carrots
Herbs
Peas
Spinach
Swiss chard

Some vegetables stay in the best condition if left on the plants until needed. This is true for hardy fall and winter crops, such as leeks and beets. However, many crops need to be picked while at their peak and will spoil if left too long. Pick these as soon as they are ready.

Vegetables and fruits are at their best when eaten as soon as possible after picking. Once picked, they continue to lose moisture by evaporation, with no opportunity to replace it from the soil. Instead of being crisp and fresh, they will soon become limp, flabby, and nowhere near as appetizing. The sugar present in vegetables such as peas also begins to be transformed into starch as soon as they are harvested from the plant; in a short time, their wonderful sweetness is lost.

Short-term storage

If it is not possible to eat crops immediately after picking, you can slow down this process of deterioration. Harvest in the cool of early morning so that the crops are filled with moisture. Put any damaged produce to one side so that any mold cannot spread. Place newly picked produce in a cool, shady, well-ventilated place as soon as possible; rinse or spray it with fresh, cold water, if appropriate.

Slow down further moisture evaporation by placing the produce in a plastic bag or wrapping it in damp paper towels; then place it in a cool pantry or the vegetable crisper in a refrigerator. Most vegetables will remain in good condition for several days like this. Leave vegetables such as beans whole instead of preparing them ahead of time. Once cut up, they deteriorate more rapidly.

Long-term storage

If you intend to keep your produce for longer than a few days—so that you can enjoy some of this summer's surplus next winter, for example—there are several methods you can use to store it.

Frozen assets: One way to store surplus fruit and vegetables is by freezing, which usually keeps them in good condition. Not all crops freeze well—tomatoes and zucchini, for example, turn mushy. However, turn them into a cooked dish, such as ratatouille, and even these awkward customers will freeze successfully. You can extend the useful life of many frozen vegetables by blanching them briefly in boiling water before freezing, which improves their long-term color and texture.

High and dry: Drying is an age-old method of storage and is good for vegetables such as shelling beans, tomatoes, herbs, and chilies. A warm, well-ventilated place is necessary for drying. The modern method is to use a special food dehydrator, which does an excellent job.

Pickles and preserves: Sugar, salt, and vinegar are all great preservatives that have been used for generations. Any good recipe book will have plenty of recipes that use a wide variety of vegetables and fruits to produce a whole range of preserves—including jellies, chutneys, and pickles—to stock your pantry shelves.

TIME SAVER

If you have a short-term abundance of vegetables that you need to freeze, and you know you'll be eating them within a few weeks, you don't need to blanch the vegetables before freezing them.

Opposite: Tomatoes are a favorite for turning into delicious homemade chutneys, salsas, and sauces. Other vegetables, such as baby onions, green beans, peppers, summer squash, and, of course, cucumbers, are all good candidates for pickling.

Picking
the winners

Thumb through a seed catalog, and you'll find yourself facing a whole crop of questions. Out of all of the different vegetables you could choose, which are the ones that will produce the best—and fastest—results? Here's where you will find out how to choose the winners in the vegetable world, along with some notable fruits and herbs.

Choosing the right vegetables

As with so many things in life, you will be more successful growing your own vegetables (and fruits and herbs) if you take a little time to plan ahead. With so many exciting and delicious-sounding varieties available through seed catalogs, it's very easy to buy a few dozen packets of seeds, only to find out later that they were not really suitable for your needs.

Family matters

First things first: only grow what you—and your family—enjoy eating. This may seem obvious, but it's surprising how many people will grow vegetables simply because they think the crops will do well and will grow quickly or because vegetables are recommended in books. However, whether it be leeks, tomatoes, zucchini, or another vegetable, there's no point in growing something that family members will not eat.

Conversely, homegrown, freshly picked vegetables can taste so much better than store-bought versions that you might change the minds of some die-hard vegetable haters. It's also fun to experiment with vegetables that nobody has tried eating before. Grow small amounts to start so that you don't waste too much precious garden space on failed experiments.

Sizing up your vegetable plot

If you have a small yard, you will probably never have enough space to grow as much food as you would like, so plan ahead when choosing seeds. Work out roughly where everything will grow, when the plants should be ready for harvesting, and which vegetables can follow after earlier ones are harvested. One good thing about fast-growing vegetables

Right: Getting your children involved in vegetable gardening when they are young is a great way to get them interested in eating vegetables. They will be more willing to try vegetables that they have proudly grown themselves.

is that you can produce more food in a smaller space.

Where you raise your vegetables will also play a big part in your choices. Climate varies greatly from one region to another. (See "Hardiness and Heat Zones," pages 34–35.) Read the seed packets carefully. (Many are coded so you can see at a glance in which areas the varieties will do well.) Don't forget to contact your local Cooperative Extension Service for information about local gardening conditions.

Individual gardens also have their own microclimates. Conditions in your garden can be different from those in the yard next door—or even from one part of your property to another. A small, sunny patio sheltered by brick walls on all sides will probably be several degrees warmer than average for the region, while a garden in a low-lying dip at the bottom of a hill can experience frost for days longer than a garden higher up the slope.

A question of time

Nearly all of the vegetables recommended in this book are easy to grow. They don't need a huge amount of fertilizing, watering, or weeding, and they don't demand difficult growing techniques or a lot of time-consuming, painstaking work. Nevertheless, keep in mind how much time you have to devote to your vegetables. If you know you have a hectic schedule, start off by growing small amounts of superfast, easy vegetables. You can always be more adventurous later on if you find you have the time to spare. Growing your own food should be fun. If it starts to turn into a chore, that's when you know you have overextended yourself.

... homegrown, freshly picked vegetables can taste so much better than store-bought versions that you might change the minds of some die-hard vegetable haters.

Above: Small raised beds are ideal for trying out new vegetables you haven't grown before. It's easier to provide care for plants confined to a small area—but soil can dry out more quickly.

Selecting the best varieties

Fast food is what this book is all about, and the vegetables (and herbs and fruits) featured in the following pages have been chosen because they are all easy to grow. Also, they won't make you wait for months before you can enjoy your harvest.

Above: Some vegetables come in an array of colors, such as this Swiss chard with white stems; other, perhaps better known, varieties have striking red stems.

Opposite: The variety you choose can affect how you grow vegetables. You can grow carrots with short roots, for example, in containers. And it's up to you when to harvest. Do you want to harvest your onions young as scallions or wait until they are mature bulbs?

The vegetables are divided into three groups according to how fast they will be ready to harvest: superfast, faster than average, and worth the wait. Their speed is not determined by how long it takes them to reach maturity, but by how long they must grow before you can start using them, which is not necessarily the same thing. Leeks, for example, take a long time to reach full size. They are traditionally sown in early to midspring, and they are not ready for harvesting until winter or even the following spring. However, you do not have to follow these traditional methods. Baby leeks are mild, sweet, and delicious, and they can be enjoyed within a few weeks of sowing, from midsummer onward. They may not be as large as fully grown, mature plants, but they are just as delicious and enjoyable.

Days to harvest

Many seed packets and catalogs provide a number for each variety that represents how many days it will take from sowing (or sometimes from transplanting) until the crop is ready for harvest. Treat these estimates with caution. The actual length of time it takes to grow the plant can vary considerably between regions and between gardens. The climate, seasonal weather, soil type, amount of fertilizer, and many other factors will affect the speed of growth. Sometimes, the number varies from catalog to catalog for the same variety. This may reflect each catalog company's experience of growing in different regions.

The "days to harvest" number on the packet may not take into account that you can harvest some crops, such as baby salad greens, at an earlier, immature stage. Fortunately, more companies are now giving maturity dates for "baby" crops, where appropriate.

Despite the inconsistencies, "days to harvest" or "days to maturity" is a useful guide to differences between varieties. In one catalog, for example, the radish 'French Breakfast' is described as maturing in 25–30 days, while the radish 'Black Spanish Round' matures in 60 days. Even if these numbers are not exact when it comes to growing these radishes in your own garden, it's obvious which variety you should choose if speed is important.

All in the details

For all of the vegetables described in this section, you will find specific guidance on sowing or transplanting, general care, and harvesting. Where appropriate, you will also find special advice on particular pests that may attack your vegetables and on plants that are suitable for growing in containers.

There is a list of recommended "favorites," vegetable varieties that have been selected for their general reliability and, above all, for their speed in being ready for harvest. These are the sprinters of the plant world, not the slowpokes. Just one word of warning: varieties come and go all the time. One season's hot favorite can disappear by the following year, so some of the varieties mentioned here may be quickly superseded. In any case, always keep an eye open for new introductions, which are often better and faster than the old stalwarts.

Superfast

These vegetables will produce some of the quickest crops possible. How fast they will be ready to harvest will depend on the conditions in your garden at the time they are growing. However, as a guide, they should all be producing an edible harvest within about five to eight weeks of sowing—and some are even faster than that.

Arugula

Also known as rocket, roquette, or rucola, arugula has been cultivated since Roman times—and has become very popular today. Since the 1990s, it has been a trendy offering at upscale food markets and chic restaurants.

Sowing and transplanting

Arugula goes to seed rapidly in hot weather, so sow it in a sheltered but lightly shaded spot. A reasonably fertile, moisture-retentive soil will produce the best results. Start sowing in early spring, and continue to sow small batches every week or so throughout the summer. Sow in rows 6 inches (15cm) apart, or scatter in patches. Arugula is often included in salad-green seed mixtures.

Care

Keep the soil moist at all times, and thin out the seedlings as they grow. As the weather cools in fall, cover the plants with cloches or floating row covers to extend the harvest period.

Below: Once the leaves are about 3 inches (7.5cm) long, they will be ready for harvesting.

Opposite: As the plant matures, arugula grows in a rosette form. It will self-seed—the seeds can be saved for up to five years.

Pest patrol

Watch out for flea beetles, which find arugula attractive and make tiny holes in its leaves. Protect the plants with a tunnel or cage of insect-proof mesh if this pest is a problem.

Arugula **pesto**

This is a variation on the classic basil pesto and makes a wonderful peppery sauce to serve with pasta, chicken, or fish. It will keep in a tightly sealed container in the refrigerator for three to four days.

Ingredients
Large bunch of arugula
1–2 garlic cloves (to taste)
Large pinch of sea salt
1/3 cup (50g) toasted pine nuts
1/2 cup (50g) grated pecorino or
    Parmesan cheese
1/2 cup (125ml) olive oil
Juice of half a lemon

Method

Remove any coarse stems from the arugula. Place the garlic cloves, salt, and pine nuts in a blender, and process until coarsely chopped. Add the arugula, grated cheese, and 1 tablespoon of the olive oil, and process again. Add the remaining olive oil and the lemon juice, and process until the pesto is the consistency you like.

Time to pick

Gather the leaves as soon as they are large enough. Either pick individual leaves as you need them, or cut all the plants close to the ground. They will regrow to provide another crop.

When the plants start to go to seed, harvest the flowering stems for eating. They generally have a mild flavor. (Taste them first—dry conditions can make them hot.) The white flowers are also edible and make a pretty addition to salads.

As the plants age, they can become unpleasantly peppery and even rank. It is best to discard the plants once they reach this stage.

Favorites

Standard arugula *(Eruca)*

- **'Adagio'** Slow to bolt, with smooth, well-flavored leaves.
- **'Apollo'** Fast growing with rounded, tender leaves and no bitterness.
- **'Rokita'** A recent introduction with attractively indented leaves. Upright and vigorous.
- **'Runway'** An oak-leaf variety, with deeply lobed foliage and a mild flavor.
- **'Skyrocket'** Good bolt resistance and attractively serrated leaves.

Wild arugula *(Diplotaxis)*

- **'Discovery'** A recent introduction, with upright, vigorous growth and a pungent flavor with a hint of sweetness.
- **'Olive Leaved'** Elongated, smooth leaves and an excellent flavor.
- **'Sylvetta'** Dark green leaves with a strong, spicy taste. Quick growing.

Wild or tame?

Most arugula varieties belong to the genus *Eruca*, but you can also find the highly prized "wild" arugula, which looks similar to ordinary arugula but belongs to the genus *Diplotaxis*. Wild arugula has a pronounced intense and aromatic flavor. Many gardeners also find it is less likely to bolt to seed than standard arugula. While not commonly available from seed suppliers, searching for it is worthwhile.

Asian greens

Apart from Chinese cabbage, there are a lot of other Asian greens that can be eaten either as salads or cooked. They add a touch of the exotic East to both your garden and your cooking, and there are many different types to try.

Sowing and transplanting

Among the many Asian greens you will find in the seed catalogs, the most popular are Chinese broccoli, choy sum, and bok choy. (Also see "Chinese Cabbage," page 87, and "Mustard," pages 94–95, another type of Asian green.) To make things more complicated, different names are often used for the same plant—you might find plants called Chinese kale, flowering greens, Japanese greens, yu choy, and celery mustard, among others. Check the pictures to make sure that you are getting what you expect.

Most Asian greens are like Chinese cabbage: they tend to bolt if grown in cool conditions during long days. Unless the varieties are listed on the seed packet as bolt resistant, sow seeds from midsummer onward. Sow all seeds thinly in an open position in moisture-retentive soil.

Care

Thin the young plants in stages to their final spacing, using the thinnings in the kitchen. Keep the soil moist at all times. Young plants are attractive to slugs and snails, so use protection if necessary. If the temperature drops after sowing, protect young plants with cloches or floating row covers.

Time to pick

You can pick most Asian vegetables as soon as the leaves are large enough to use, either as baby greens for a salad, or when they are

Above: Once the plants begin to compete for space, thin out the smaller ones and use the leaves for salads.

Opposite top: Bok choy, one of the most popular of Asian greens, forms a vase-shaped head that can be cut with a sharp knife when ready for harvesting.

Edible chrysanthemum

Most Asian greens are members of the cabbage family, but there is one that is different: the garland chrysanthemum, also known as shingiku, tong ho, and choy su green. A member of the chrysanthemum family, its leaves have a distinctive aromatic flavor that intensifies as the plant grows. It is best eaten young, either raw or briefly cooked, because the leaves can become bitter with age.

Favorites

Chinese broccoli: Also called "Chinese kale" or "gai laan," it produces tender flowering stems and blue-green leaves.

- **'Crispy Blue'** Fast growing, with stalks ready for picking in about seven weeks. New shoots continue producing to give a long season.
- **'Green Lance'** An F1 hybrid with uniform, vigorous growth. Ready in six to seven weeks.

Choy sum: Similar to Chinese broccoli, with slender, tasty flower stems, often red or purple in color.

- **'Hon Tsai Tai'** Attractive purple stems and flower buds, with a mild, spicy mustard flavor. Bolt resistant.
- **'Tsoi Sim'** Tender green leaves and stems in about six weeks.

Bok choy: Produces heads with broad, crisp white leaf stalks and tender, bright green leaf blades.

- **'Joy Choi'** Slower to mature than 'Toy Choi' at about seven–eight weeks, but larger plants with succulent white leaf stalks and deep green leaves.
- **'Toy Choi'** A dwarf hybrid, quick to crop at about four–five weeks.

larger, for cooking. Bok choy will produce neat, plump heads if you let the plants mature. They generally require about 8 to 10 weeks to form.

You can also pick the leaves of Chinese broccoli and choy sum, but these plants are usually harvested when they produce flowering shoots. Cut the shoots when young, while the flower buds are tightly closed and the stems are still tender. Bok choy also produces edible flower stems.

Name	Row spacing	Plant spacing
Chinese broccoli	12 inches (30cm)	12 inches (30cm)
Choy sum	18 inches (45cm)	9 inches (23cm)
Bok choy	18 inches (45cm)	6 inches (15cm)

Broccoli rabe

A member of the cabbage family, broccoli rabe is more closely related to turnips than broccoli. It produces flowering heads that resemble broccoli, but it's ready for harvesting much more quickly. It is also known as broccoli raab, rapini, and broccoletti.

Sowing and transplanting

For an early harvest, sow broccoli rabe in pots indoors in late winter or early spring, setting the young plants out after the risk of frost is over. Transplant carefully, disturbing the roots as little as possible to avoid bolting.

It is more common to sow broccoli rabe directly where it will grow, from midspring to late summer. Sow small amounts in batches about three to four weeks apart for a long harvest season. In hot weather, the plants may bolt quickly, so in warm areas it is often better to take a break from sowing between late spring and midsummer. However, many gardeners report that plants continue to grow successfully, despite the heat.

Sow the seeds thinly, aiming to space them 1 inch (2.5cm) apart in rows 6–12 inches (15–30cm) apart. Wider spacing will produce larger plants, so adjust the spacing according to variety and how you want to use the plants.

Care

Thin the young plants in stages to 4–8 inches (10–20cm) apart, using the thinnings as salad greens or as cooked greens. Keep the soil moist at all times, especially in hot weather. Because the plants grow so quickly, they are usually pest and disease free.

Time to pick

Plants mature quickly, from as early as 30 days after sowing—and they will race past their prime harvest time if you are not careful.

Cut the flowering stems as soon as they appear. In just a day or two the whole head will probably open into full flower and no longer be edible. Don't worry if just one or two yellow flowers have opened within the head—the heads are still perfectly edible at this stage. The flowering shoots will keep well for several days in a plastic bag in the vegetable crisper of a refrigerator.

Good eating

Eat the leaves and stems as well as the flowering shoots. All parts of the plant have a spicier flavor than broccoli, with a mustardlike heat. Cook the stems by steaming or boiling lightly until just tender, or by stir-frying. You can either leave the stems whole or chop them, according to taste. Thicker stems may be a little tough at the base—test by snapping the stems to check that they break cleanly. If they seem tough, peel the bases with a vegetable peeler. If you do not like the slight bitterness of broccoli rabe, blanch the stems in boiling water for a minute to sweeten them before stir-frying.

Favorites

- **'Cima Di Rapa'** A popular plant of Italian origin, reliable and with a good flavor. Frilly, fresh green leaves.
- **'Sessantina Grossa'** This broccoli rabe has thick stems and a bluish tinge, more like ordinary broccoli.
- **'Serranto'** An early broccoli rabe that is fast to mature with heavy yields.
- **'Sorrento'** Large florets on a fast-maturing plant, giving good yields.
- **'Zamboni'** Uniform plants with a good, spicy flavor and relatively large heads, but a little slower to mature than other varieties.

Opposite: Broccoli rabe is ready for harvesting as soon as the florets appear—and before the buds open into full flower.

Kale

One of the hardiest members of the cabbage family, kale will survive in the garden throughout the coldest weather—it will provide green or purple-tinted leaves for picking even under snow and ice. However, you don't have to wait until winter to enjoy a harvest from these versatile plants.

Above: Kale thrives in moist, fertile soil. The young, tender leaves have a more subtle flavor that makes them ideal for salads.

Sowing and transplanting

Kale needs a moist, fertile soil to grow well. Sow the seeds thinly in rows 8–10 inches (20–25cm) apart if you want to harvest the whole crop as baby leaves, or up to 18 inches (45cm) apart to leave some plants to continue growing. Start sowing in midspring, and continue making small sowings every two weeks or so for harvesting as baby leaves.

Care

Keep plants well watered. A high-nitrogen liquid fertilizer in early summer encourages them to produce plenty of tender leaves. Thin plants in stages to leave them 18–24 inches (45–60cm) apart if you want to retain plants for harvesting through fall and winter.

Pest patrol

Cabbage aphids are destructive. These are small, gray-green, waxy-coated pests found in clusters on leaves. Curly-leaved kale varieties have plenty of hiding places, so if aphids are a problem in your garden, choose the plain-leaved kale types. Aphids will be easier to spot and wash off the leaves.

Time to pick

Harvest kale grown for salad greens when the seedlings are 3–4 inches (7.5–10cm) tall, or pick individual leaves from young plants. Continue to pick leaves from the plant throughout the winter.

Good eating

Young leaves are the most tender and tasty; older leaves can be tough and bitter, especially in salads. To use kale leaves raw, remove the midrib, which can be fibrous. When too tough for salads, shred the leaves and steam, boil, or stir-fry them. Blanching leaves in boiling water for a few minutes before stir-frying removes some of the bitter flavor that can develop.

Favorites

- **'Dwarf Siberian'** Frilly-edged, green and purple leaves.
- **'Lacinato'** An Italian kale with strap-shaped, puckered, and blistered blue-green leaves. It is sometimes referred to as "dinosaur kale."
- **'Red Ursa'** Broad, frilly-edged, purple-tinged leaves of good flavor and tenderness. Young leaves can be used for salads even when picked from mature plants.
- **'Starbor'** An F1 hybrid producing compact plants with bright green, frilly-edged leaves.
- **'Winter Red'** A plain-leaved Russian type that many people find best for eating raw. The red color intensifies with cold weather.

Chinese cabbage

Quick-growing Chinese cabbage is versatile—the crisp, firm heads can be eaten raw or cooked and have a pleasant, mild flavor. There are several types of Asian cabbages, but the term "Chinese cabbage" usually means the barrel-shaped napa varieties.

Sowing and transplanting

Chinese cabbage likes rich, fertile, moisture-retentive soil. Its main problem used to be that it would bolt early in cool weather and long days, so it had to be sown from midsummer onward, when it was reliably warm and days started to get shorter. Modern varieties are much less likely to bolt than older ones, but check the variety description on the seed packet to make sure you pick one suitable for spring sowing.

Sow the seeds thinly in rows 12–18 inches (30–45cm) apart. Ideally, the temperature should be above 60°F (16°C) to avoid bolting, but bolt-resistant varieties can cope with temperatures as low as 50°F (10°C). For an early harvest in cool areas, sow the seeds indoors in individual pots or modules; then plant the seedlings outdoors once the weather warms up. Be careful not to disturb the sensitive roots when transplanting.

Care

If there is a sudden cold spell after sowing, use cloches or a floating row cover to protect the sowing area and the seedlings as they appear. Thin the seedlings to 8–12 inches (20–30cm) in the row—you can use the thinnings as salad greens. Keep the soil moist at all times because Chinese cabbage is a thirsty crop. Fertilizing with a liquid, high-nitrogen fertilizer will help to keep the plants growing fast, especially in less fertile soil.

Sow small amounts of seeds every two or three weeks for a succession of heads. Once the plants reach a reasonable size, they will bolt quickly, so be sure you avoid having a lot of plants maturing at the same time.

Time to pick

You can harvest the leaves as soon as they are large enough. To harvest a whole head, squeeze it gently to see how solid it is. If firm, cut the head at soil level using a sharp knife. Don't delay cutting, or the plant will soon go to seed. (You can still harvest and eat the individual leaves, even if a plant starts to seed.)

Although Chinese cabbage will not keep for long in the garden, once cut it will keep well in a cool place or in the vegetable crisper of a refrigerator for several weeks. Use the leaves as you would use regular cabbage, such as in stir-fries, salads, and even coleslaw.

Favorites

- **'Blues'** Slow to go to seed, the dense, bright green heads with clean white ribs are produced in about eight weeks.
- **'Mini Kisaku 50'** Small, tight heads with crisp, creamy yellow centers. Ready to cut in about seven weeks.
- **'Minuet'** Neat, small, tightly packed heads form seven weeks from sowing.
- **'Orient Express'** A reliable cabbage with good bolt resistance; small, solid heads are ready for harvest in about six weeks.
- **'Qinmeng Spring'** Heavy heads form in about eight weeks. Bolt resistant and suitable for spring and fall harvests.
- **'Tenderheart'** A miniature cabbage ideal for a single serving and suitable for pots; it matures in about seven weeks.

Above: Most vegetable gardeners usually let Chinese cabbage form a tight, barrel-shaped head before harvesting.

Cress

The leaves of cress have a pleasantly peppery flavor, making them a perfect choice if you want to spice up a green salad. There are two types of cress commonly grown: upland cress and garden cress. Both are quick and easy to grow.

TIME SAVER

When watering cress, use a fine spray attachment to prevent the low-growing leaves from getting splashed with soil. Cress needs only a quick rinse before it is ready to eat.

Above: As upland cress grows larger, the intensity of the "bite" in the outside leaves increases. Pick these first; when the outer leaves become unpleasantly hot, start harvesting leaves from the center of the plant.

With dark green, spicy-flavored leaves, upland cress looks and tastes similar to watercress. When it comes to growing them, however, there's a difference. While watercress is usually difficult for gardeners to grow because it prefers growing in running water, upland cress is more amenable. Garden cress, also known as peppergrass, is the simplest cress to grow. Generations of young children have been introduced to growing their own food by sprinkling seeds of this cress onto damp washcloths or paper towels and watching the seedlings shoot up. Both types of cress are commonly included in mesclun seed mixes.

Sowing and transplanting

Upland cress likes moist soil and a lightly shaded position, away from the heat of the summer sun. Sow in rows 8 inches (20cm) apart, and thin the seedlings gradually to leave plants 6 inches (15cm) apart. Garden cress likes similar conditions. Instead of sowing them in rows, broadcast the seeds. (Scatter the seeds over the ground.)

Start sowing both types of cress early in spring. The leaves can turn unpleasantly spicy in hot weather, so in warm areas, take a break from sowing between early and midsummer. Upland cress is reasonably hardy, and a late-

Cress throughout winter

Garden cress is easy to grow on a windowsill or in any bright place indoors all through the winter, even without a pot.

Fold a sheet of paper towel twice so there are four thicknesses of paper. Place it in an empty, clean plastic container or on a saucer. Moisten the paper towel with water, draining off the surplus after it has absorbed all it can. Sprinkle cress seeds thickly on the paper towel, and place in a warm, well-lit position.

The seeds will absorb the water and form a gel-like coating, which protects them from drying out. Add a little water to the paper towel, if necessary, as the seedlings grow, and then cut them as soon as they are tall enough.

A fun way for children to grow cress is to make a stencil of the child's name and sprinkle the seeds onto the paper towel through the stencil.

summer sowing will produce leaves for picking into the early winter.

Plants for pots

Garden cress is an obvious candidate for container growing, but upland cress also does well when sown directly in containers. Water the cress regularly to keep the potting mix moist at all times, otherwise the leaves can become unpleasantly hot to the taste.

Care

Thin young upland cress plants to about 4 inches (10cm) apart. Keep the soil moist, giving a thorough watering every 10 days or so, more frequently in dry weather. Garden cress does not need thinning, because it is cut as seedlings. Sow small patches about every 10 days for a succession of harvests.

Time to pick

Cut seedlings of garden cress when they are about 2 inches (5cm) tall, using a pair of sharp scissors. Pick leaves of upland cress from the outsides of the plant as soon as they are large enough, or you can harvest the whole plant by cutting it down almost to the ground. It should regrow to produce another crop.

Favorites

Upland cress (*Barbarea verna*)
- Named varieties are not usually available, but there is an attractive variegated form sometimes sold as 'Variegated Winter'. This has pale cream-and-green mottled leaves.

Garden cress (*Lepidium sativum*)
- **'Cressida'** Plain, serrated leaves, quick growing.
- **'Greek cress'** Curly-leaved cress with a particularly intense flavor.
- **'Presto'** Bright-green leaves, ready to cut in 10 to 12 days.
- **'Wrinkled Crinkled'** Bright-green, heavily ruffled leaves. Slightly slower than other varieties, but all garden cress is ready to cut within three weeks.

Above: When harvesting individual leaves of upland cress, pick them at the base of the leaf, being careful not to pull the whole plant out of the ground.

Mesclun

Sowing and transplanting

Most of the plants grown as mesclun prefer moderate temperatures. Conditions above 77°F (25°C) can lead to problems with germination and premature bolting. In warm areas, sow seeds from early spring, take a break over the hottest weeks, and start sowing again in late summer, when things have cooled down. In temperate regions, choose a lightly shaded spot for sowings in midsummer.

Mesclun seeds are usually sown in blocks instead of rows, sprinkling the seeds thinly over the soil and raking it lightly into the surface. Sow patches at about 10-day intervals for a succession of harvests.

You can buy prepared mixtures of mesclun, or you can create your own mix by buying separate packets of seeds. The prepared mixtures may consist of a single packet of mixed seeds or small amounts of separately packeted seeds; separate packets of seeds allow you to tailor the quantities of each constituent to your own taste.

If you make up your own mix of mesclun to grow together, check the packet to be sure they have a similar seed-to-maturity time. Otherwise you'll be harvesting the plants at different times.

The colorful mixture of young leaves known as mesclun, or misticanza, has become popular in recent years. Its wide variety of flavors, textures, and colors makes a salad that is much more exciting than the plain old lettuce of years gone by.

Plants for pots

Mesclun mixes are ideal for pots. You will want to harvest a reasonable quantity of leaves at one time for a meal, so pick a container that has a suitably large surface area. It does not need to be deep.

Above and opposite: Salad greens are perfect for growing in containers, either as a mixture of varieties together (above) or as individual varieties. Choose varieties by shape and color to create your own striking container planting (opposite).

Origins of mesclun

Mesclun originally comes from the Provence region of France, where the traditional mix is arugula, chervil, lettuce, and endive. The word is derived from the Latin *misculare*, meaning "to mix."

Amaranth

Swiss chard

Young lettuce

Spinach

Beet

Basil

Favorites

These are just a few of the mesclun mixtures available from seed companies:

- **Tangy Blend** Lettuce 'Red Sails', lettuce 'Nevada', arugula, Batavian endive, joy choi.
- **Mild Blend** Kale 'Dwarf Siberian', lettuce 'Slobolt' and 'Red Sails', mâche, mizuna, mustard 'Tah Tsai'.
- **Niche Mix** Leaf radish, leaf carrot, wrinkled cress, 'Red Russian' kale, red amaranth, golden purslane, salad burnet.
- **Connoisseur's Mix** Red-stem leaf radish, kale 'Dwarf Blue', lettuce 'Red Cos', lettuce 'Green Oakleaf', chop suey greens, chicory 'Italico Rosso', saltwort.
- **Cut-and-Come-Again Lettuce Mix** Lettuce 'Rouge Grenobloise', 'Royal Oakleaf', 'Cimarron', 'Red Salad Bowl', 'Batavia Blonde'.
- **Insalata Odorosa Mix** Curly and escarole endives, chicory, lettuce, mâche, erba stella, cutting celery, arugula, pimpinella, cress, borage, chervil.
- **Cook's Tangy Mix** Japanese mustard, arugula, Dutch broad-leaved cress, red and green Italian chicories.
- **Classic Mesclun Mix** Arugula, chervil, endive, mâche, lettuces 'Oak Leaf', 'Prizeleaf', 'Red Salad Bowl', and 'Green Ice', radicchio, upland cress.

Care

These quick-growing crops need little in the way of care, except for keeping the soil moist at all times. Cover the area with cloches or floating row covers early and late in the season to protect the plants from cold weather. Thin out seedlings if the plants become overcrowded—use the thinnings in salads.

Pest patrol

If you find ragged holes in the leaves, the most likely culprits will be slugs and snails. Look for their telltale slimy trails. Carry a flashlight, and handpick these pests when they are most active at night. If you prefer not to handpick them, set up slug traps to control any invaders. (See "Fighting Off the Enemy," pages 64–65.)

Time to pick

The easiest way to harvest mesclun is to wait until the young plants are large enough to eat; then completely cut down a patch big enough for your needs using a pair of sharp scissors. Leave stumps about 1–2 inches (2.5–5cm) tall, and within two or three weeks they should regrow to provide another harvest. In good conditions, you can cut the area a third time before the plants are exhausted. A high-nitrogen liquid fertilizer after each cutting will help stimulate strong regrowth.

Experiment with cutting the plants at different stages of growth to see what produces the best results. Very young leaves are sweet and tender. Leaving the plants until they are slightly larger will often provide more intense and aromatic flavors and increase the total crop. However, do not let these plants grow for so long that they become tough and fibrous.

Try to cut mesclun mixes in the early morning. Rinse them under cold water; shake them dry; and store them in a plastic bag in the vegetable crisper of a refrigerator. While they will keep for a day or two, they are much better eaten the day they are picked.

Plants suitable for mesclun

Amaranth
Arugula
Basil
Beet
Celery
Chervil
Chinese cabbage
Chives
Cilantro
Cress
Dandelion
Edible
  chrysanthemum
Endive
Kale
Lettuce
Mâche
Mizuna
Mustard
Oregano
Parsley
Radicchio
Salad Burnet
Scallions
Spinach
Swiss chard

Mustard

Usually found listed among Asian vegetables in the seed catalogs, the many varieties of mustard have become popular both for salads and cooking. They have a spicy bite that ranges from mild to intensely hot, depending on the variety and the stage of growth of the plants.

Mizuna and mibuna

These are not true mustards but have a similar flavor and are often listed as mustards in seed catalogs. They produce attractive, rosette-forming plants with narrow leaves and white or purple leaf stems. The foliage of mizuna is serrated and feathery, while mibuna has rounded, less feathery leaves. Both have a mild, spicy mustard flavor, with mibuna having the stronger flavor of the two. Mizuna is tolerant of cold and makes a good winter salad green if given the protection of cloches or floating row covers.

Sowing and transplanting

Rich, moisture-retentive soil and a sheltered, sunny position suit mustard well. Sow seeds from midspring. Like many other Asian vegetables, cold weather and long days can cause the plants to bolt to seed, although modern varieties tend to be more bolt resistant. In cool areas, sow the seeds in modules under cover, and grow them in a minimum temperature of 65°F (18°C) until the young plants are ready to be planted outside—this will help to prevent them from bolting. You can continue to sow mustard seeds through late summer.

If sowing seeds outside, sow them in rows 12–18 inches (30–45cm) apart and thin the plants to 6–12 inches (15–30cm). Plant transplants outdoors at similar spacing.

Care

Thin the young plants in stages until they reach their final spacing. Keep the soil moist at all times; mustard plants have shallow roots and are vulnerable to drought. Dry soil conditions will make the leaves hotter to the taste; water thoroughly and regularly for a milder crop.

Above: Mustard leaves grow in a variety of shapes, colors, and sizes, from the variegated leaves of this mustard 'Red Giant' to smooth green leaves to curly purple leaves.

Opposite: The leaves of some larger varieties, such as this mustard spinach, might require a sharp knife to harvest them.

Time to pick

Harvest young plants whole, or pick leaves as needed for salads as soon as they are large enough. As the plants are thinned out and grow larger, cut a few leaves at a time from the outside of the plant.

If the plants start to bolt, you can use the flowering shoots and stems either raw or cooked; however, they can be spicy. Spring-sown crops are the best choice to use as baby leaves. Let the seedlings sown in mid- to later summer form larger plants because there is less chance of them bolting than earlier sowings.

Mustards are generally most useful as part of a mixed-leaf salad, where they add bite to less assertive greens.

Favorites

- **'Florida Broad Leaf'** Tall plants with large, deep green leaves. A vigorous grower.
- **'Green Wave'** Forms an upright plant with deep green, curly-edged leaves. Good bolt resistance.
- **'Komatsuna'** Also known as mustard spinach, this plant has smooth, tender leaves and good bolt resistance.
- **'Red Giant'** The large, textured, purple-maroon leaves have a strong flavor and are decorative, particularly in cold conditions when the color intensifies. Quick growing.
- **'Savannah'** A quick-maturing F1 hybrid with broad, smooth leaves.
- **'Tendergreen'** A popular mustard with smooth, succulent leaves that have a mild flavor. Quick growing; best sown in late summer because it has a tendency to bolt when sown earlier.

Table mustard

Mustard is one of the most ancient condiments. The species of mustard greens described here (*Brassica juncea*) produces brown seeds; these are mixed with black or white mustard seeds and ground to a fine powder to produce mustard flour. Mustard flour's bite is released only when it is mixed with a cold liquid; its pungency is reduced by any form of heating. Mild, American-style mustard uses mainly white mustard seeds (*Sinapsis alba*) mixed with vinegar and sugar. English-style mustard, made from the stronger brown mustard seeds, is stored as dry powder and mixed with cold water just before each use. It has an intense flavor.

Radish

Only seed sprouts can really beat radishes as speedy vegetable crops. Crisp, tender roots are ready for pulling just three or four weeks from sowing. There are many types in a range of colors and shapes, and all will liven up your salads.

Sowing and transplanting

Don't be tempted to sow too many radish seeds at once. They quickly become coarse and woody, so make small, regular sowings about every 10 days. Sow seeds as soon as you can rake the soil in early spring, sprinkling them thinly along rows 6 inches (15cm) apart. The plants are not particular about soil, sun, or shade. However, keeping the soil moist will help to prevent the roots from becoming unpleasantly hot, so moisture-retaining soil is generally best.

In hot climates, take a break from sowing when the weather starts to warm up in late spring; then start sowing again when the worst of the summer heat is over.

Plants for pots

Quick-growing, shallow-root radishes are perfect for pots and containers, such as window boxes. Most types are suitable, but avoid long-root types, such as 'White Icicle'.

Above: Once the seedlings begin to appear, you may need to thin them—use the extra seedlings as a salad green.

Center: Small, red, globular radishes are the most common, but some types produce larger cylindrical roots. In general, choose radishes with small roots because these take the shortest time from sowing to maturity.

Care

No special care is necessary—simply pull the young roots as soon as they become large enough to eat. Keep the soil moist during dry spells; this will help to keep the radishes crisp and sweet. If you sowed the seeds too thickly, thin the seedlings out as they develop. Overcrowded plants will not form well-shaped roots.

Pest patrol

Not many pests will bother with radishes, except for flea beetles. They seem to have a passion for radish leaves. If you find the leaves peppered with tiny holes, run your hand gently over the top of the foliage down the row while watching closely—you will probably see tiny black beetles pinging into the air.

These beetles are only a problem if you intend to eat the leaves. Covering the row with insect-proof mesh right after sowing the seeds is the best preventive measure.

Summer and winter radishes

Summer radishes are the type with which we are most familiar, producing round or long roots in shades of pink, white, and red. There are also winter radishes, sometimes known as daikon. These produce large, coarse roots that take much longer to grow. You can grate or cook daikon radishes before eating. Summer radishes are the ones to choose if you want speedy vegetables.

Waste not ...

Radishes grow so quickly that if you turn your back for a few days, they will be past their best and sending up flower shoots. Don't worry: let these plants flower and set seed; then harvest the pods while they are still young and tender. Radish pods taste like snow peas but with a punchy bite.

Good eating

If you have too many radishes, try sautéeing them for a few minutes in butter or olive oil. They make a tasty side dish.

Favorites

- **'Cherriette'** An F1 hybrid that matures quickly in just three weeks. Round, cherry red roots.
- **'Cherry Belle'** Round, smooth, scarlet roots with crisp, white flesh. Quick to reach maturity.
- **'Fire 'N Ice'** Elongated roots with red tops and white tips. Crisp texture and a mild flavor.
- **'Plum Purple'** Deep, plum pink, round roots. This radish has good heat tolerance.
- **'Sparkler'** Round, bicolor roots, red with white tips.
- **'White Icicle'** Long white roots with crisp flesh and a mild flavor.

Time to pick

Pull the roots as soon as they are large enough to eat. If you need to thin out the plants to provide enough space for the roots to develop, add the young leaves to salads. Harvest the roots as soon as they are ready, even if you do not intend to use them immediately. They will keep better in the vegetable crisper of a refrigerator than they will in the ground. Rinse them under water to remove the soil. Twist off the leaves, but leave the stems, cutting them off only just before you serve the roots.

Above: Choose a short-root radish to grow in a container, and make sure you keep the soil moist as the vegetables grow.

Seed sprouts

Whether you grow seed sprouts or microgreens, you'll find them to be the quickest and easiest crops you'll ever grow. They are ready to eat within days, and you can grow them throughout the year—even in the darkest, coldest days of winter. There's a huge range of colors and flavors available to spice up your salads and stir-fries.

Above right: Only the tender young leaves and stems of microgreens are harvested. The flavor of both microgreens and sprouts will vary, depending on which seeds you grow. Experiment with different types to find the ones you prefer.

Opposite: Mustard-seed sprouts are just one of the many varieties that you can grow at home—they are delicious in salads and sandwiches.

Sowing

There are different types of seed-sprouting kits available, but the easiest (and cheapest) of them all is a simple glass jar. Wash the jar thoroughly with plenty of hot, soapy water; rinse well, giving it a final rinse with boiling water. Rinse the seeds thoroughly; then cover the bottom of the jar with a thin layer. A 1-quart (450g) jar takes about a tablespoon of seeds, but this varies according to their variety. Cover the seeds with water. Make a strainer by cutting a piece of cheesecloth to fit the top of the jar, and hold it in place with a rubber band. Let the seeds soak for about eight hours or overnight. Strain off the soaking water, and rinse and drain twice daily until the seeds have sprouted sufficiently for you to eat.

Most store-bought sprouting kits consist of stacking, slatted plastic trays. These are good for growing several varieties of sprouts in a compact space. However, harvesting them can be difficult because the roots grow through the slats, making the trays awkward to clean.

Care

You can put the jar in a dark place for white sprouts or in the light for green ones. Try both methods to see which you prefer—each has a slightly different flavor and texture. After rinsing, leave the jar on its side or with the bottom propped up so that any remaining water will drain away from the seeds.

Time to pick

The seeds will begin sprouting within a few days, and within another two to six days, depending on the variety, they will be ready to eat. All you need to do is remove them from the jar after rinsing.

You can often take out half of the young sprouts to eat at an early stage and continue to rinse and drain the remainder for another couple of days. They will soon bulk up to fill the jar. If you want to store the sprouts for a day or two, let them dry off for a few hours after rinsing, and then store them in a plastic bag in the refrigerator.

Favorites

- **Adzuki beans** Sweet, nutty sprouts.
- **Alfalfa** Small, yellow-green shoots with a sweet, raw-pea taste.
- **Amaranth** Mild flavor and bright red color. Good as microgreens.
- **Arugula** Best sown as microgreens. Sweet, spicy flavor.
- **Broccoli** Hot, spicy flavor. Good choice as microgreens.
- **Buckwheat** Delicate, sweet flavor, similar to lettuce. Use hulled seeds for sprouts; grow unhulled seed as microgreens.
- **Cabbage** Mild mustard taste. Red varieties make attractive sprouts.
- **Chervil** Subtle aniseed flavor when grown as microgreens.
- **Chickpea** (garbanzo) Firm, crunchy texture and mild flavor.
- **Cilantro** Grow as microgreens; strong flavor.
- **Clover** Similar to alfalfa, with a sweet, raw-pea taste.
- **Cress** Familiar, peppery taste. Best as microgreens.
- **Fennel** Anise flavor and feathery shoot. Good as microgreens.
- **Fenugreek** Spicy curry flavor and aroma.
- **Lentil** Subtle, peppery taste. Many different varieties available. High in protein.
- **Mung beans** The best-known sprout, chunky with a crisp texture.
- **Mustard** Flavor varies from mild to hot and spicy.
- **Onion** Mild onion taste. The black seed coats can be hard.
- **Peas** Sweet shoots with a nutty texture; snow peas are the sweetest tasting.
- **Radish** Spicy, mustardlike flavor. Red- or white-stem varieties are available.
- **Sunflower** Mild, nutty taste. Hulled seeds are best because the seed coats are tough.

Microgreens

Microgreens differ from seed sprouts because once the first leaves appear, they are harvested by cutting the stems and leaving the seeds and roots behind. This method has been used for years to grow mustard and cress but is now popular for other seeds, too. Microgreens have an intense flavor but are more tender than sprouts because you are not eating the seeds.

Sow seeds for microgreens in seed-starting mix or on a burlap sack, washcloth, or even paper towels. Depending on which material you use, the germinating seeds will often leave their seed coats behind, which some people prefer. It is a good way to grow mucilaginous seeds, such as arugula or cress, which form a gooey gel on contact with water and can be messy.

Sprout safety

There has been some publicity about seed sprouts involved in outbreaks of food poisoning. However, these were commercially produced sprouts, where the risk of contamination is much greater than with homegrown sprouts. Whenever food is concerned, it is sensible to take basic precautions. Use only seeds sold as suitable for sprouting; other seeds may be contaminated or have been treated with chemicals.

Thoroughly wash the equipment used for sprouting, and use clean, fresh water for rinsing the growing sprouts.

Not all seeds are suitable for sprouting, particularly large beans, such as kidney beans. These contain toxins that are only destroyed by prolonged heating. In any case, the sprouts of large beans are not particularly tasty. There are mixed reports on soybeans, but it is safer not to sprout them, because they can cause digestive problems.

Turnip

A versatile vegetable, the turnip provides not only crisp, sweet roots in a range of shapes and colors but also a bonus of vitamin-rich greens from the leafy tops. They are quick and easy to grow and have a long season.

Care

Thin the seedlings in stages to 4 inches (10cm) apart, using the thinnings as greens. Keep the soil moist at all times, especially in hot weather, to keep the plants growing quickly to produce sweet, crisp, tender roots.

Pest patrol

Flea beetles can be a particular problem on turnips grown for their leafy tops. This small pest makes numerous little holes over the surface of the young leaves. Protecting the plants with an insect-proof mesh row cover is the best prevention.

Time to pick

Pull the young roots as soon as they become large enough to eat. For salads, most varieties are sweetest and most tender at 1–3 inches (2.5–7.5cm) across. Let roots for cooking grow to 4–6 inches (10–15cm). Check the seed packet descriptions because some varieties claim to stay crisp and sweet at larger sizes.

Cut turnip tops for greens when they are about 6 inches (15cm) tall, leaving a stump that is about 1 inch (2.5cm) above ground level. The tops should regrow to produce an additional harvest. You can harvest younger leaves for salads. Some varieties are dual purpose and will produce both greens and tasty roots, but other varieties selected for their leafy tops will not produce a usable root. Most turnips have bristly, hairy leaves, but some selections have smooth foliage.

Sowing and transplanting

While turnips are not a temperamental crop, they prefer reasonably cool conditions and plenty of moisture. A fertile, moisture-retentive soil will produce the best-quality roots. In warm areas, sow in a lightly shaded place, and avoid sowing when the crop will mature during the hottest weather of the summer. Excessive heat can make the roots pithy and unpalatable.

Turnips are cold-hardy plants, so you can start sowing in early spring. Continue at intervals throughout the summer and into fall. Sow thinly in rows 6–9 inches (15–23cm) apart. If you are growing the plants for the green tops, sow them at the closer spacing. Turnips sown in fall will overwinter to produce a crop of greens in early spring.

Favorites

- **'Hakurei'** Dual-purpose turnip with smooth, white, flattened roots that have a sweet, fruity flavor. The greens are hairless.
- **'Hinona Kabu'** Unusual Japanese turnip with long, slender, carrotlike roots, white with a scarlet top.
- **'Milan'** Flattened roots with a red top and pleasant "buttery" flavor. An all-white selection is also available.
- **'Scarlet Ohno'** A dual-purpose turnip with flattened, red-skin roots and smooth, hairless leaves, often with a red tinge.
- **'Scarlet Queen Red Stems'** Crisp white-and-pink flesh with a colorful cherry red skin. A dual-purpose turnip, the hairless, deep green leaves have attractive red stems.
- **'Seven Tops'** Grown for its tender green tops, the woody roots are inedible.
- **'Shogoin'** Dual-purpose turnip with globe-shaped white roots and tender, mild-flavored greens.
- **'Snowball'** Popular and reliable, with smooth, globe-shaped white roots.
- **'Tokyo Market'** Dual-purpose turnip with smooth, hairless leaves and sweet white roots. Quick growing.
- **'Topper'** Abundant crops of tasty, deep-green tops. You can eat the roots, though they are slow to mature.

To store the roots, leave 2 inches (5cm) of the tops attached to the roots; keep them moist inside plastic bags; and refrigerate.

Good eating

If you have childhood memories of tough, fibrous, watery chunks of boiled plain, overlarge turnips, it may have turned you against eating them. Try them like this: leave the young roots whole if small enough, and dice or slice any larger roots. Place the turnips in a saucepan with just enough water to cover, a large pat of butter, a couple of teaspoons of brown sugar, and 1–2 tablespoon of balsamic vinegar. Season to taste with salt and black pepper, and cook over medium heat until the turnips are tender and the liquid has reduced to a tasty glaze.

Opposite: If cabbage worms are a problem in your garden, cover turnips and other cabbage-family plants with netting to keep egg-laying butterflies at bay.

Left: The roots may be globular, such as these, or they can be cylindrical, flat, or oval. Which variety of turnip you choose may depend more on whether you want to grow it for the roots or leaves—or both.

Bush bean page 104

Pole bean page 106

Beet page 108

Carrot page 110

Cutting celery page 112

Kohlrabi page 114

Baby leek page 116

Lettuce page 118

Mâche page 122

Potato page 128

Scallion page 132

Spinach page 134

Faster than the average vegetable

Choose the right varieties of the vegetables in this group, and you should be able to start harvesting them within 8 to 12 weeks after sowing, depending on where you live and what the weather is like in any particular season. All of these vegetables require relatively little attention, so they won't put your patience to the test.

Pea page 124

Swiss chard page 136

Bush bean

Whether you want snap beans, shell beans, or dry beans, you can grow all of them as easy-growing bush beans. These compact plants provide good crops of crisp, tender beans all through the summer—and the beans freeze well for winter use, too. There are numerous varieties from which to choose, and you will find beans in several colors, including yellow and purple.

Below: Bush beans are attractive plants for hanging baskets, especially if you choose a variety with yellow or purple beans—they will also be easier to see among the green leaves.

Opposite top: Pick snap beans when young and fresh. Test when they are ready by picking a pod and trying to bend it in the center. If it snaps crisply in half, the beans are ready to harvest.

Opposite bottom: Raised beds with high edging material can help provide support for beans grown in an exposed site.

Sowing and transplanting

Bush beans like warm, sheltered conditions and a reasonably fertile, moisture-retentive but free-draining soil. Sow them outside from late spring after all danger of frost has passed. The soil temperature for germination needs to be at least 50°F (10°C). You can sow seeds from midspring under cloches, or a little earlier in pots indoors. Make fresh sowings every 10–14 days for a season-long supply. Space the seeds 2–4 inches (5–10cm) apart in rows 18 inches (45cm) apart. Plant container-sown plants outside at the same spacing in early summer.

Plants for pots

An early crop of tasty bush beans is worth growing in containers. The beans will be free of the soil splashes and slug damage that can ruin crops from plants in the ground. Set one plant in a 12-inch (30cm) pot that is at least 12 inches (30cm) deep. Keep the plants well watered, and feed with a liquid fertilizer, such as a tomato fertilizer, once the plant starts flowering.

Care

Most bush beans do not need any support. However, on exposed, windy sites, you can provide them with some branched brush along the row after sowing. (See "Supporting

Getting to know the bean family

Trying to decipher the many terms used when referring to beans can be a challenge. *Phaseolus vulgaris* is the species covered in this book. The main difference between the two types is how they grow. Bush beans are compact plants known as determinate, which means they stop growing after they reach a certain size and have produced blossoms and the pods. Pole beans are indeterminate. These vinelike plants keep growing and producing a crop. Both bush beans and pole beans produce snap beans, shell beans, and dry beans, which are the beans at different stages of maturity. Young and tender snap beans are eaten whole, both pod and seeds; green beans, string beans, and French beans are all snap beans. Shell beans are swollen, mature beans, eaten fresh without the pods. Dry beans are left on the plant until the seeds are hard and have shrunk; then you store the beans for winter use. Snap beans are the ones to grow for the earliest harvest.

Roles," pages 56–57.) This will prevent the plants from leaning over so that the beans touch the soil, which makes them both more difficult to pick and more likely to be damaged.

Once flowering starts, water the plants to improve the setting of the pods and keep plants cropping. Watering before flowering (unless it is dry) will tend to produce bushy, leafy plants with fewer flowers. The earliest varieties will start cropping about seven weeks from sowing.

Pest patrol

There's an impressive list of insects that are attracted to beans, including aphids, flea beetles,

Favorites

- **'Contender'** Heavy crops of rounded pods with a good flavor.
- **'Fin De Bagnols'** French-filet type with slender pods. Early cropping and good flavor.
- **'Gold Mine'** Early cropping, sweet golden beans on compact, upright plants.
- **'Greencrop'** Flat, Italian-style pods of fine texture and flavor.
- **'Jade'** Produces long, straight, stringless dark-green pods that are sweet and tender.
- **'Provider'** Reliable early variety with round, fleshy pods.
- **'Purple Queen'** Deep-purple beans, easy to see when picking, turn rich green when cooked.
- **'Storm'** Straight, crisp, round pods. Early maturing.
- **'Triumphe De Farcy'** Quick to crop, with slender, round pods.

Mexican bean beetles, leafhoppers, leaf miners, and whiteflies. Many of these can be held at bay by protecting your plants with floating row covers.

Time to pick

Start picking pods just as soon as they are large enough. Frequent picking encourages further pods to form. Hold onto the plant's stem with one hand while you pull off the bean with the other; bush beans have shallow roots, so it is easy to loosen the plant in the soil or even pull it out altogether by tugging too hard.

Good eating

Beans have the most taste when eaten fresh, but you can store them for several days in the refrigerator. Rinse the beans, if necessary, and store them in a plastic bag. Trim off the stalk end before cooking—there is no need to remove the thin "tail" at the other end. Cook in boiling water for a few minutes until they are just tender.

Pole bean

These climbing beans take a little extra work because they need supports, but they produce one of the heaviest crops of all vegetables in relation to the ground space they require.

Below: Pole beans are vining plants, and without support they will scramble over the ground.

Opposite top: Pole beans will provide a bumper crop of fresh, tender beans, well worth the little bit of extra effort to provide them with supports.

Opposite bottom: An A-frame support will provide plenty of growing space for pole beans.

Sowing and transplanting

Like bush beans, pole beans like warmth and will not germinate in cold soil. (See "Bush Bean," pages 104–105.) Covering the soil with cloches or sheets of black plastic to keep it dry will help to warm the soil sooner in the spring, letting you sow an early crop. You can also sow pole beans in pots indoors and plant them outside once the weather is warm enough. If you live in an area where diseases are a problem, look for cultivars with built-in resistance or tolerance. Seed catalogs often use codes for these, including bean common mosaic virus (BCMV), curly-top virus (CTV), anthrocnose (A), and bean rust (R).

Set the supports in place before sowing or planting the beans. This ensures that the roots won't be damaged, something that can occur if the stakes are put in place after the plants begin to grow. The plants will also have support as soon as it is needed. There are various methods for supporting pole beans, such as a frame supporting string, netting, or wire. (See "Supporting Roles," pages 56–57.)

Perhaps the easiest method, particularly in a small garden, is to make a tepee. Pole beans grow to 6 feet (2m) or more, so to make a tepee, buy stakes 7–8 feet (2–2.4m) tall. Depending on the amount of space you have, make a tepee of four to eight stakes, pushing them firmly into the soil at a slight inward angle and then bringing the tops together and tying them with strong garden twine.

Experiments have found that providing about 1 square foot (9cm²) of space for each plant produces good yields, so keep this in mind when arranging your stakes. For example, a tepee with a base diameter of 3 feet (1m) can contain seven stakes 16 inches (40cm) apart, with one plant to each stake. However, a practical arrangement of stakes that provides easy access to the plants for picking is the most important consideration.

Care

If you use smooth bamboo or plastic stakes, twist some rough twine around the bottom third of each stake to give the young plants something to grip as they start climbing. You can help them get started by gently twisting the young stems around the supports. Be sure you twist them in the right direction, or they will unravel themselves—look at some of the other shoots to check which way they are twining. Pinch off the tips of the shoots once they reach the top of the supports.

Favorites

- **'Blue Lake Pole'** A heavy crop of round, mid-green beans. There is also a bush variety by this name.
- **'Kentucky Blue'** An early hybrid with round, sweet pods.
- **'Kwintus'** An early pole bean, quick to mature, with long, flat green pods. Long season and heavy yields.
- **'Marvel of Venice'** Pale-yellow, flat pods on a vigorous plant. The white-seed form is quicker to provide a crop than the black-seed strain.
- **'Neopolitan Pole'** Long, flat, tender pods with good flavor.
- **'Northeaster'** One of the earliest pole beans. Long, wide, flat pods with good flavor.
- **'Romano'** Long, flat, light-green pods with good flavor.

Beans must have plenty of water once flowering starts because this helps pod setting and development. Apply the water to the roots. As the season progresses, feeding with a high-potassium liquid fertilizer helps to keep the plants in production.

Pest patrol

Black aphids sometimes colonize the young shoots of plants and can stunt their growth. Inspect the growing tips regularly, and either pinch off the affected tips or wash off the clusters of aphids with a strong jet of water.

Time to pick

Pick the pods as soon as they are large enough to eat, and pick them often to keep the crop going. If the pods mature and develop seeds, it will signal to the plant that it is time to stop flowering. Look carefully among the foliage, especially where it is crowded at the top of the supports, so that you don't miss maturing pods. If you find that you have enough of the fresh, young snap beans, you can leave the remainder to mature and use as shell beans or dry beans.

Many bean varieties are described as stringless, but on larger pods you may want to remove the stringy margins with a sharp knife before cooking.

Favorites

- **'Blankoma'** Slightly conical, pure white roots. Mild flavor.
- **'Boro'** An F1 hybrid with smooth, dark red roots.
- **'Bull's Blood'** Grown for its maroon, wavy-edged leaves, used young in salads, but it also produces tasty roots.
- **'Carillon'** Ideal for young baby beets. Sweet and high yielding.
- **'Chioggia'** A novel beet with a pink-and-white "bull's-eye" root. Steam or roast to preserve the colors.
- **'Early Wonder'** Fast, dual-purpose beet with scarlet, globe-shaped roots.
- **'Kestrel'** An F1 hybrid with smooth, round, dark-red roots of sweet flavor.
- **'Little Chicago Hybrid'** Good dual-purpose beet with a fine flavor.
- **'Touchstone Gold'** Dual-purpose plant with tasty leaves and sweet golden flesh that does not bleed.

Beet

Beets are best known for their sweet, earthy-tasting roots, but you can eat the leaves, too. The roots are usually a rich purple-red, but white or gold beets are available—and there are even bicolors with concentric rings of white and magenta. All beets have edible foliage, but some have more-tender, milder-tasting leaves than others; these are often described as dual-purpose beets.

Sowing and transplanting

Sow beets from midspring, sowing small batches every two weeks or so for a succession of crops. Beet seedlings will bolt if they are subjected to temperatures of 50°F (10°C) or below for two weeks or more. In cool areas, delay sowing outside until the weather is warm enough. In warm areas, take a break from sowing a few weeks before the hottest weather is likely, and start sowing again once the worst of the summer heat is over.

Alternatively, for early crops, sow the seeds indoors in seed-starting trays for planting outside later. Unlike many root crops, transplanting does not appear to stimulate bolting in beets, although you should try to keep root disturbance to a minimum. Transplants are a better option for gardens with clay soil, where seed germination is often poor. If you buy young started plants, there will be the additional bonus of not needing to thin out the plants at a later stage.

Soaking seeds in tepid water for several hours will improve germination rates by washing away some of the natural inhibitors in the corky seed coat. Space the seeds 2 inches (5cm) apart in rows 7 inches (18cm) apart for the heaviest crop of baby beets. Set transplants about 4 inches (10cm) apart.

If you want only baby beet leaves for salads, sow the seeds more thickly, and harvest whole plants as soon as they are large enough to eat, which is usually before the roots expand.

Plants for pots

Baby beets grow well in pots. Sow the seeds about 1 inch (2.5cm) apart, and thin the plants as they develop.

Care

Thin the seedlings to 4 inches (10cm) apart, using the leaves of the thinnings for salads. Keep the soil evenly moist to prevent the roots from cracking, which can happen when heavy rain or heavy watering follows dry weather. If there is a cold spell once the seedlings have emerged, protect plants with cloches or floating row covers.

Time to pick

The roots are both fastest and tastiest when gathered young as baby beets—when they are no more than 1–2 inches (2.5–5cm) across. Twist off the leaves, and handle the delicate roots carefully to avoid damaging them. It will also help to prevent their color from bleeding when they are cooked.

Good eating

Boil the roots until they are tender, and serve them either hot or cold. They are a popular choice for pickling. You can also grate baby beets and eat them raw—they have a strong, sweet, earthy flavor.

Young leaves are delicious in salads. Cook the older greens as you would spinach. They taste similar to Swiss chard.

Opposite: When digging up beets, handle them gently. If you use a fork, be careful that you don't accidentally spear a root in the process.

Carrot

Sweet, tender baby carrots are real family favorites. Short-root varieties are less fussy about soil and quicker to grow than the longer types, so they are ideal for gardeners in a hurry.

TIME SAVER

Look for pelleted carrot seeds. These are much easier to sow thinly and will save time thinning the young carrots later.

Above: For the best results, carrots need loose, stone-free soil. Check the plants occasionally to make sure they are not growing too closely together, and thin out as needed.

Opposite: Carrots with short roots will do well both in the vegetable plot and in containers.

Sowing and transplanting

Light, free-draining soil without stones is best for carrots. Turn over the soil well to be sure there is not a hard layer of compacted soil a few inches below the surface. Compacted soil will stop roots in their tracks and result in some strange, forked carrot shapes. Stony soil will have the same effect.

Carrot seeds are slow to germinate and need a minimum soil temperature of 46°F (8°C). For an early sowing in spring, place cloches or floating row covers over the area where you want to sow in late winter to help warm the soil. Sow the seeds as thinly as possible in rows 6 inches (15cm) apart. (See "Pest Patrol," below.)

Plants for pots

If you choose the right variety, carrots make good container plants. Look for short-root carrots, such as 'Little Finger', or the globe-root 'Parisian Market'. The container should be at least 8 inches (20cm) deep. Keep the potting mix evenly moist all the time the carrots are growing.

Care

Thin the young plants to 4 inches (10cm) apart, using the thinnings as baby carrots when large enough. Keep the soil slightly moist, but do not overwater. Carrots grown in fairly dry conditions have the sweetest, most concentrated flavor.

If the shoulders of the developing roots protrude above the soil, use a hoe to mound the soil up to cover them. Exposed tops turn green and can be bitter.

Pest patrol

Carrot flies ares small black insects that skim over the soil surface and lay eggs in the developing root. These hatch into white maggots that tunnel their way through the carrots and can ruin the crop. Because they do their dirty work below-ground, the first sign of trouble is usually a failure of the plant to thrive and a distinctive rusty-red discoloration of the foliage.

The flies are attracted to the plants by scent, so avoid disturbing or bruising the leaves. Sowing the seeds thinly will help to keep the thinning of the seedlings to a minimum. Any weeding or thinning necessary should be carried out at dusk, when the flies have minimal flying time to find the crop. A 2-foot-high (60cm) barrier of insect-proof mesh erected at ground level all around the carrot-growing area will help to keep carrot flies out because they fly at ground level. Look for

the cultivars 'Resistafly' and 'Flyaway', which have been bred for their resistance to carrot fly attack.

Time to pick

Start pulling roots when their tops reach ½– ¾ inch (12–18mm) across. In light, moist soil, the roots can be pulled by hand, but in heavier soil or in dry conditions, ease them up with a fork to prevent the brittle roots from snapping.

Good eating

Wash away the soil clinging to the roots under running water—there is no need to peel young carrots, and unpeeled roots have a more intense flavor. The youngest carrots can be eaten raw; if cooked, boil until just tender.

Favorites

- **'Amsterdam 2'** A sweet baby carrot, with uniform, deep-orange roots 3–4 inches (7.5–10cm) long.
- **'Little Finger'** Popular, quick-growing, tender miniature carrots.
- **'Mignon'** Smooth-textured, rich-orange baby roots.
- **'Minicor'** Quick growing, ideal for baby carrots. A small core keeps the flesh tender and sweet, with an intense flavor.
- **'Mokum'** Quick-growing, slender carrots with a good flavor.
- **'Parisian Market'** Globe-shaped roots, ideal for shallow soil or containers.
- **'Shin Kuroda'** An early Japanese short-root carrot with an excellent sweet flavor.
- **'Short 'N Sweet'** Short, chunky, tapering roots good for heavy or poor soil. Sweet flavor with a deep-orange color through to the center of the root.
- **'White Satin'** An unusual pure white carrot with a sweet, mild flavor. Keep the tops covered with soil to prevent them from turning green.

Cutting celery

Standard celery is a difficult and time-consuming plant to grow well, but if you hanker after its flavor without all the hard work, then cutting celery is for you. Cutting celery, which is a variety of celery, is also known as leaf celery, soup celery, and smallage. All parts of the plant are strongly aromatic.

Sowing and transplanting

The seeds are slow to germinate and need soaking in water for a few hours or overnight before sowing. You can sow them in pots indoors in early spring and plant them outdoors in midspring. Alternatively, sow the seeds directly in the soil outside from midspring onward. Allow 6–9 inches (15–18cm) spacing for each plant.

Plants for pots

Because you only need small quantities of cutting celery to add to your salad greens mix, this is a good plant for growing in a small container.

Care

Cutting celery is an undemanding grower, but it likes reasonably fertile, moisture-retentive

Allergy alert

Celery has been known to cause allergic reactions in sensitive people, so be careful when introducing it into your diet, especially if you are prone to other allergies. Contact with celery plants can also cause dermatitis (a type of skin inflammation), especially in sunny weather. This usually affects only people who handle large amounts of celery, but those with sensitive skin should keep their hands and arms covered when working with celery plants.

Right: Cutting celery is a herb with a strong flavor, so just one or two plants will usually be ample for most home gardens.

Lovage: A celery substitute

Although its leaves and stems have a strong celery flavor, lovage is not a type of celery. It is a tall, stately perennial herb, and its young shoots are among the first to poke through the herb garden soil after the winter. Lovage likes a sunny or lightly shaded spot, and in rich, moisture-retentive soil it will easily grow to 5 feet (1.5m) high and about half as much across, so give it plenty of space. The leaves can be used just like cutting celery.

soil and an open, sunny position. Although cutting celery can be overwintered in most areas (using cloche protection against severe frost), it is a biennial and will go to seed rapidly in its second year.

Time to pick

Cutting celery grows to 18 inches (45cm) high and has slender stems and parsleylike leaves. You can harvest both the leaves and stems as soon as they are large enough. A single plant will provide a good supply of leafy stems on a "cut-and-come-again" basis.

After the plants flower in their second year, you can harvest the seeds to use as a seasoning, too—they have the same pungent celery flavor.

Good eating

Use cutting celery in soups and casseroles, either by chopping and adding to the dish or by adding a small bunch of whole stems during cooking and removing them before serving, as you would a bouquet garni. You can add the leaves to salads. The flavor is pungent, so be careful to avoid adding too much. Mix a small amount of seeds with salt in a grinder for a tangy celery-salt seasoning.

Favorites

This plant is most often listed simply as cutting celery or leaf celery in catalogs (or Chinese celery from Asian seed suppliers), but a few named varieties are available.

- **'Amsterdam'** A neat, compact celery with deep-green leaves.
- **'Da Taglio'** An Italian celery producing strong, upright-growing plants with deep-green leaves.
- **'Safir'** Tall, sturdy plants with a strong, aromatic flavor. Regrows quickly after cutting.
- **'Tianjini Green'** Chinese celery with a strong flavor.
- **'Zwolse Krul'** ('Par-cel') Often described as a cross between parsley and celery in flavor, this selection has frillier, more finely cut leaves than the standard type.

Favorites

- **'Eder'** Extra-fast maturing, with tender white globes.
- **'Express Forcer'** A fast-maturing plant with tender, crisp globes. Good for warm areas because it is heat tolerant.
- **'Grand Duke'** Good-quality pale-green globes. Quick to mature.
- **'Kolibri'** An F1 hybrid that resists becoming woody. Deep purple with smooth white flesh; a fast-growing purple kohlrabi.
- **'Kongo'** Uniform white globes; quick to reach usable size, with a mild, sweet flavor.
- **'Rapidstar'** As its name implies, an early kohlrabi, quick to crop. Pale-green globes.
- **'Sweet Vienna'** Smooth, crisp texture. An improved, fast-maturing version of 'White Vienna', a long-established kohlrabi.
- **'Winner'** Heavy-yielding green kohlrabi, resistant to woodiness.

Kohlrabi

It may look like a turnip, but kohlrabi is not a root vegetable—its pale-green or purple globes are actually swollen stems. If you pull them young, when they are sweet and tasty, you can enjoy them either raw or cooked.

Sowing and transplanting

Kohlrabi is not selective about soil, but it will grow best in reasonably fertile, free-draining conditions. It likes an open, sunny position.

Sow the seeds from early or midspring, but wait until the temperature is at least 50°F (10°C) because cooler conditions can cause plants to bolt to seed prematurely. Sow the seeds thinly in rows 12 inches (30cm) apart. Sow small batches every 10–14 days for a succession of young plants. The globes may be purple or pale green, but the flesh inside is white no matter what the skin color. (The green varieties tend to be quickest growing.)

Care

Thin the seedlings to 4–8 inches (15–20cm) apart, being careful not to disturb the roots of the seedlings that are left in the row. Keep the soil moist at all times. The plants need to grow quickly and without any disruption to their growth to produce the sweetest and most tender crop. Regular watering is important as the summer weather heats up.

Pest patrol

Kohlrabi is a member of the cabbage family. It is prone to attack by insect pests that attack this family, such as the cabbage maggot, imported cabbageworm, cabbage looper, and flea beetle. Placing insect-proof mesh over the rows after sowing is the best way to keep pests at bay. If your plants are attacked by the cabbage maggot, grow kohlrabi (and other cabbage family plants) in a different place the next year. The pest overwinters in the soil and will attack a following crop.

Opposite: As a cabbage-family member, it's not surprising that kohlrabi has a mild sweet flavor similar to cabbage and turnips.

Children's favorite

Its strange appearance, resembling a Russian sputnik or an alien craft from outer space, makes kohlrabi a good choice for getting children interested in growing their own vegetables. They will also be impressed by its speedy growth. Make sure that you serve children kohlrabi when the globes are young and tender, before their cabbagelike flavor becomes too pronounced.

Time to pick

Pull kohlrabi when the globes are about the size of a golf ball. Although modern varieties tend to stay sweet for longer, it is best not to let them get much bigger than a tennis ball. Large globes are often unpleasantly woody or pithy inside. Hot weather accelerates the rate at which they go past their best. There are one or two cultivars that are specially bred to remain usable when much larger, but these are not the fastest-growing plants, so they don't fit into the "fast-food" category.

Good eating

You can eat young globes complete with their skin, but generally it is best to peel them because the skin can be tough. For eating raw, most people prefer kohlrabi grated, but it can also be sliced or diced. Grated kohlrabi makes a good base for coleslaw, particularly when mixed with grated apple—these flavors complement each other well. You can cook kohlrabi in various ways; try it steamed, stir-fried, or sautéed.

The leaves of kohlrabi are also suitable for eating. You can cook them as you would any other cabbage green.

Baby leek

Succulent, mild leeks are often grown as a hardy vegetable that stays in the garden through the winter. However, baby leeks are much quicker and easier to grow. Choose early varieties, and you will be pulling bunches of tender young leeks throughout the summer and fall.

Sowing and transplanting

Sow baby leeks directly where they will grow in the ground, sowing the seeds thinly in rows 8 inches (20cm) apart. You can also broadcast them in 2–3-inch (5–7.5cm) bands. Sow seeds in succession every 10–14 days for a season-long supply.

For an early crop, sow seeds indoors in a seed-starting tray in early spring. Transplant the seedlings outdoors when they are about 3–4 inches (7.5–10cm) tall. Leeks transplant well, so you can sow them in trays or a spare area in the garden throughout the spring and summer and move them once space becomes available after harvesting another crop.

Plants for pots

With their compact, upright growth, leeks make good plants for containers. Either sow seeds directly in the container, or plant young transplants about 3 inches (7.5cm) apart.

Care

Thin young plants to 3–4 inches (7.5–10cm) apart—you can use the thinnings in the same way as you would scallions. Keep the soil moist as the plants are growing.

When transplanting seedlings, trim the spidery roots using scissors to reduce them to a neat fringe, and drop each seedling into a deep hole made with a dibble. Space them 3–4 inches (7.5–10cm) apart. Trickle a little water into the hole to wash down enough soil to just cover the roots. Planting the leeks deeply blanches the stems to make them extra tender and mild.

Right: The roots of seedlings removed from pots for transplanting can become entangled and need trimming.

Opposite: You can leave some leeks to mature and pick other leeks young, providing you with a supply throughout the summer and fall and into winter.

Time to pick

Harvest the young leeks as soon as they are large enough to use—about the same size as scallions. If you want to have some larger leeks, leave a few plants 6 inches (15cm) apart to continue growing. If you intend to leave some leeks in the ground for use as a winter vegetable in cold areas, make sure you choose a completely hardy variety. Providing a straw mulch will help protect them against frost.

Good eating

Trim the roots and tops of the leeks, and wash them well to get rid of any grit that has become trapped in the wraparound leaves. You can eat young leeks raw, but they are usually cooked. Because young leeks are tender, they cook quickly—be careful to avoid overcooking them. They are usually eaten whole and are particularly good when braised with a little stock. You can also roast or sauté young leeks, but first blanch them in boiling water for two to three minutes; then drain thoroughly.

Favorites

- **'Baby Primor'** Fast-maturing French leek especially bred for using as baby leeks. Tender texture; sweet with a good flavor. Hardy.
- **'Electra'** Hardy leek suitable for baby or full grown leeks.
- **'Jolant'** Quick-growing leek with a mild flavor. Not reliably hardy.
- **'King Richard'** Light-green leaves and sweet, smooth-textured flesh. Not reliably hardy, but more heat tolerant than many varieties, so good for hot regions.
- **'Lancelot'** Mild flavor with deep blue-green leaves. Hardy.
- **'Lincoln'** Slender, tall, upright leek. Not hardy.
- **'Varna'** Quick-growing leek with long, slender stems. Not hardy.

Lettuce

Cool, crisp lettuce is the mainstay of summer salads. There are dozens of types and varieties to grow, in a range of colors, textures, and leaf shapes. Sow little and often, and you will have lettuce to enjoy all through the summer and into winter.

Sowing and transplanting

Most lettuce varieties prefer cool growing conditions. Lettuce seeds become dormant in soil temperature of 77°F (25°C) or above, which can be a problem for summer sowings. In hot regions, choose a position that is lightly shaded to help extend summer sowings. Select varieties carefully because some are more heat tolerant than others. You may need to take a break from sowing in the hottest months.

The soil should be moisture retentive and reasonably fertile. Water the bottom of the furrow before sowing, and sow the seeds in early or midafternoon so that they reach the critical stage of the germination process at night, when it is cooler.

Sow seeds in shallow furrows in rows 9–15 inches (23–38cm) apart, depending on the variety. For a succession of harvests, sow the seeds in small batches, making the next sowing as soon as the previous batch of seeds germinate.

Below: Growing different varieties of lettuce will give you a selection for more interesting salads.

Right: Sow seeds thinly when planting in a container, and cover with a thin layer of soil. Make sure the soil stays moist.

Opposite: If the top 2 in. (5cm) of soil gets dry, it's time to water lettuce, especially in hot weather.

Care

Thin the young plants in stages to 6–10 inches (15–25cm) apart, using the thinnings in the kitchen. It is important to keep the soil moist at all times.

Plants for pots

You can grow looseleaf and compact romaine lettuce successfully in a range of containers, where they will be easier to keep slug free than when growing in the ground. You can also move containers to a shady position on hot, sunny days.

Time to pick

Start picking looseleaf lettuce as soon as the leaves are large enough. For "cut-and-come-again" crops, pick the leaves individually from the outsides of the plants, leaving the center to continue growing. If you prefer, you can harvest whole plants by cutting the head, leaving a stem of about 1 inch (2.5cm) or so behind, which will sprout again.

Cut heading varieties when they have formed a firm heart; test them with the back of your hand to avoid bruising the leaves.

Lettuce quickly goes to seed in hot weather, so you should cut them as soon as they are at their peak. Once they start to bolt, the leaves turn bitter and are inedible. Romaine varieties do not go to seed as rapidly as butterhead types. You can store cut lettuce in the refrigerator for a few days.

Lettuce types

Looseleaf: If you want fast food, this is the group to concentrate on—these are the first lettuce to be ready for harvesting. They form a loose rosette of leaves that you can harvest from the outside in a cut-and-come-again fashion. Some varieties will form a heart if you let them develop; however, they do not form as densely as other lettuce types.

Butterhead: Soft yet crisp, butter-heads produce succulent leaves that have a silky texture. The outer leaves are dark green and coarser than the inner leaves, which fold over themselves to form a dense yellow heart. Bibbs are a small type of butterhead that are much prized for their flavor.

Romaine: Popular for Caesar salad, these have an upright, sturdy habit of growth and crisp leaves with a firm, wide midrib. Romaine lettuce is also known as cos. This can be one of the sweetest lettuce, and the leaves may be either smooth or ruffled.

Crisphead: This is a tightly packed lettuce that produces crisp, inward-curling leaves that wrap around to form a dense, succulent head. Iceberg lettuce is one of the best-known types. Crispheads are a more difficult type to grow and are the slowest type of lettuce to produce a usable crop.

Lettuce continued

Favorites
Looseleaf

- **'Black Seeded Simpson'** A cut-and-come-again lettuce with crisp, wavy-edged leaves. Continues cropping throughout summer and into fall.
- **'Merlot'** Deep-red leaves, upright grower. Cold hardy.
- **'Red Sails'** Bronzy-red, ruffled leaves. Heat tolerant, so good for warm areas.
- **'Salad Bowl'** Cut-and-come-again lettuce with deeply lobed leaves. **'Red Salad Bowl'** is a red-leaf selection.
- **'Slobolt'** Dwarf, compact cut-and-come-again lettuce with mild, crisp leaves. Bolt-resistant plant.
- **'Verde Ricciolina'** Quick-growing Italian lettuce that has tender, curled, and ruffled leaves.

Butterhead

- **'Burpee Bibb'** Sweet flavor, with soft, pale heads. Not recommended for hot areas.
- **'Buttercrunch'** Dense head formed by broad, green leaves; buttery texture.
- **'Dancine'** Baby butterhead with small, dense heads.
- **'Focea'** Quick-maturing miniature heads with a sweet flavor and buttery texture.
- **'Four Seasons'** Cold-hardy small, neat lettuce that, as its name implies, you can grow throughout spring, summer, and fall, and even into winter with some protection. Attractive, red-tinged leaves.
- **'May Queen'** One of the earliest lettuce, with medium, pale-green heads.
- **'Optima'** Large, dense heads formed by deep-green leaves with a velvety texture and good flavor.
- **'Pirat'** Tender leaves with a good flavor. Outer leaves tinged red.

- **'Skyphos'** Large, deep-red heads with contrasting green centers. Quick growing with a good flavor.

Romaine

- **'Amaze'** Small, neat heads with shiny maroon outer leaves.
- **'Dazzle'** Mini lettuce with deep-red leaves forming a good heart. Fast growing and ideal for containers.
- **'Ez Serve'** Small, dense heads that fall into separate leaves from the base; quick to prepare for eating. Mild flavor.
- **'Freckles'** Glossy, mid-green leaves with attractive maroon splashes.
- **'Green Forest'** Bolt resistant, forming a tall head of tender leaves. Heavy yielding.
- **'Little Gem'** A favorite at the table, and easy to grow. Small, neat heads with a dense heart.
- **'Little Leprechaun'** Upright, green and bronzy red leaves that form a tightly wrapped, medium heart.
- **'Super Jericho'** Good heat resistance, remaining sweet and crisp during hot summer days.

Crisphead

- **'Crispino'** Fast-growing lettuce with medium, firm heads.
- **'Igloo'** Crispy heads that form quickly but stay in good condition for a long time, even in hot conditions.
- **'Red Iceberg'** Deep, maroon-edged leaves that quickly form medium heads. Resistant to bolting.
- **'Summertime'** Does well even in hot summers. Light-green, medium head surrounded by frilly outer leaves.
- **'Tiber'** Large, round, firm heads of tightly wrapped, deep-green leaves.

Looseleaf lettuce

Romaine lettuce

Butterhead lettuce

Crisphead lettuce

Mâche

This salad green is hardy and can survive winter in most areas. Mâche, which is also known as corn salad and lamb's lettuce, grows as a neat rosette. It has a mild but pleasant and distinctive flavor, and the leaves have a succulent, buttery texture.

Sowing and transplanting

Sow the seeds from early spring right through early fall. Sow in a reasonably fertile, moisture-retentive soil in an open position, either by broadcasting the seeds in patches or sowing them in rows 4–6 inches (10–15cm) apart.

Sow batches every 10–14 days for a succession of harvests. In warm areas, take a break from sowing about four weeks before the highest temperatures are expected, and resume when

The tale of Rapunzel

This German fairy tale is about a man and his wife who have longed for a child for many years. At last the wife is pregnant. One day she spies some lush green leafy plants growing in the garden next door, which belongs to an enchantress. The pregnant woman develops such a strange and powerful craving for the plants that she becomes certain she will die unless she eats some. Her husband, therefore, sneaks into the enchantress's garden every evening after dark to gather the plants for her. One night the enchantress finds him. In a fury, she threatens him with a terrible fate for stealing from her garden. The terrified man begs for mercy, promising to give the enchantress anything she desires, which turns out to be their newborn baby girl. The enchantress calls her Rapunzel, whisks her off to live locked up in a tower deep in the forest, and we all know the rest of the story.

What was the plant that provoked such an overwhelming desire in the pregnant woman? At least some versions of the story say it was mâche. Try it, and see if you develop a hankering for it, too.

the hottest weather is over. In hot conditions, mâche goes to seed quickly.

Plants for pots

Mâche is a suitable candidate for growing in containers and often forms part of a mesclun mix for baby salad greens. Its mild flavor produces a pleasant contrast to the spicier, hotter flavors of other baby salad greens.

Care

Thin the plants, if necessary, using the thinnings in the kitchen. Keep the soil evenly moist. In midfall in cool areas, cover the plants with cloches to keep the leaves in good condition through the winter.

Time to pick

Harvest the entire rosette by cutting off the head just above ground level. The plant may regrow to produce another crop. Or remove individual leaves as needed and let the plants keep growing.

The low-growing leaves need thorough rinsing to remove soil splashes, but use a gentle spray of water to avoid bruising them. They will keep for a few days in a plastic bag in the refrigerator. However, the outer leaves quickly turn slimy, so it is best to cut only as much as you need for a meal and use it right away.

Favorites

- **'Bistro'** Quick growing, with deep-green leaves of a velvety texture and sweet, buttery taste.
- **'Cavallo'** A productive plant with a mass of fresh, deep green leaves.
- **'D'Etampes'** Round leaves that are flatter than other varieties, without the cupping at the tips.
- **'D'Olanda'** Large-leaved mâche, resistant to bolting.
- **'Jade'** Heat tolerant, with elongated leaves.
- **'Large Seeded Dutch'** Particularly large, lush leaves.
- **'Macholong'** Hardy and productive, with bright green leaves.
- **'Piedmont'** Large, pale-green, spoon-shaped leaves. Productive plant.
- **'Verte de Cambrai'** A well-established, cold-tolerant mâche that is excellent for winter production.
- **'Vit'** Reliable plant with succulent, fresh green leaves.

Opposite: Because mâche can take longer to grow than other greens used in a mesclun mix, it is better to grow it in a separate container and add to the mix at harvest time.

Above: Mâche will retain its mild flavor, even after it matures or goes to seed, making this a good choice for the garden.

Pea

Sweet, young peas are among the most delicious crops a gardener can grow, and there's a great range of types from which to choose. If you pick the varieties carefully, you will enjoy a harvest sooner than you might think.

Sowing and transplanting

Start sowing the seeds in early spring, using a quick-maturing, early variety. Continue with additional sowings until around midsummer. In some areas, a fall-sown crop of a hardy variety will overwinter to produce one of the earliest harvests next summer, but this is only worth trying in light, free-draining soil and where the winter is not too severe. The plants will survive frost but not extended low temperatures.

Peas are traditionally sown in bands about 6 inches (15cm) wide, either scattering the seeds thinly across the width of the band or sowing a double row along the edges, spacing the seeds about 2–4 inches (5–10cm) apart.

Care

To help the plants grow and crop better, provide supports for peas, even for the bush varieties that are claimed to be self-supporting. Tall varieties definitely need

Below: You can put more-permanent types of support, such as wire mesh stretched between stakes, in place before sowing the seeds to ensure that you don't damage seedlings.

Right: Once the pods are approaching maturity, visit the plants often so that you can pick them at their peak.

Wrinkles are **sweet**

Pea seeds are either smooth or wrinkled, and this difference is important to gardeners. Wrinkles give seeds a much larger surface area, but this is not necessarily a good thing. In wet conditions, this means more of the seed surface is in contact with water. In cold, wet weather, this makes wrinkled pea seeds more likely to rot than smooth pea seeds. For the earliest sowings of the year, smooth pea seeds are far more likely to succeed.

However, wrinkled pea seeds produce peas with a much sweeter flavor than peas from smooth seeds. (They have a better balance of starch and sugar within the pea.) So for later sowings, where rotting is not such a problem, choose wrinkled pea-seed varieties for the best flavor.

larger the peas grow, the more starchy and less sweet they become. Pick snow peas while the peas are still tiny and unformed and the pods are flat and about 2–3 inches (5–7.5cm) long. You have a choice when it comes to harvesting snap peas. Pick them immature as you would snow peas, or wait until the peas arc a similar size to those of shelling peas, with the pods round but still bright green and smooth. As with shelling peas, if you let snap peas become too large inside the pod, they will lose their sweetness.

Below: Peas are attractive plants to grow in the garden. Here, a picket fence provides support.

support. Providing supports will also make the pea pods easier to harvest. To avoid damaging the plants, put supports in place before sowing; you can use netting, stakes and string, or brush. (See "Supporting Roles," pages 56–57.)

Wet soil slows down root development, so avoid watering seedlings. Once the flowers start to appear, water the plants during dry spells. Make sure the water goes to the roots; keep it off the leaves by applying the water directly to the soil.

Time to pick

Pick shelling peas when the peas inside the pods are plump and well rounded but before they are packed tightly within the pod. The

Types of pea

Shelling peas: Also called "garden, English," or "green peas," pick shelling peas when the peas in the pods are completely round but still young and tender. Shell the peas out of the pods, and discard the pods. *Some varieties produce small, sweet peas called "petit pois."*

If you prefer, you can leave shelling peas on the plant to mature completely so that they become dried or split peas, a pantry staple that needs to be soaked before cooking.

Snow peas: The French name *mangetout*, meaning "eat all," tells you what you need to know about this type of pea—the entire pod is eaten. You must pick snow peas at the right stage—before the peas within the pod become enlarged—or the pods will be stringy and tough.

Snap peas: Also called sugar snaps. Like snow peas, the entire pod is eaten, but unlike snow peas, the peas inside can develop until they are the same size as shelling peas. The pod remains sweet, juicy, and virtually stringless. Modern snap-pea varieties have plump, succulent, thick pods and were first bred in the 1960s, though some snap-pea varieties were grown centuries ago.

Good eating

Eat shelling and snap peas as soon as possible after picking, because the sugars will start to turn to starch as soon as the pods are removed from the plant. Snow peas often need to be stringed before they are cooked. You can do this by using a sharp knife to cut away the tip and then pulling away the fibrous strings with it. Snap peas are not normally stringy unless they are left on the plant too long, in which case you may need to run a sharp knife around the edges of the pod before cooking. Eat snow peas and snap peas either raw or cooked.

Favorites

Shelling peas

- **'Caselode'** Short, well-packed pods. Peas are slow to turn starchy.
- **'Dakota'** Early pea, quick to mature, with long pods of sweet peas.
- **'Feisty'** Compact vines produce a lot of tendrils but few leaves, making harvesting easier. Sweet peas and tasty tendrils, ideal for garnishing.
- **'Little Marvel'** Compact plants with blunt, dark-green pods packed with sweet peas.
- **'Premium'** Early, with sweet, medium peas on a compact plant.
- **'Spring'** Fast growing with dark pods, an early harvest plant.
- **'Sprint'** Early plant producing flavorful, sweet, small-to-medium peas.
- **'Strike'** One of the earliest, with mid-green, flavorful peas.
- **'Waverex'** Productive *petit pois* variety. Small peas with a sweet flavor.

Snow peas

- **'Dwarf Grey'** Small, high-yielding plant, both heat and cold tolerant.
- **'Dwarf White Sugar'** Quick to produce a heavy crop of sweet, tender pods, which are stringless when picked early.
- **'Little Sweetie'** An early, quick-growing, compact variety with stringless pods.
- **'Snow Sweet'** Pods remain tender and sweet for longer than many snow-pea varieties.

Snap peas

- **'Cascadia'** Short, compact plants with large, dark-green pods.
- **'Sugar Ann'** Compact, bushy plants with a heavy crop of crisp pods. Early.
- **'Sugar Bon'** Delicious, sweet pods produced on compact plants.
- **'Sugar Sprint'** Heavy crop of virtually stringless pods. Heat tolerant.
- **'Sugar Star'** Early and strong growing, with dark-green pods on compact plants.

Shelling peas

Snow peas

Snap peas

Potato

If you are used to store-bought potatoes—one of the most well-known food staples—wait until you taste freshly unearthed new potatoes from your own patch. There's nothing to match their wonderful flavor and texture. For a quick-growing crop, choose early varieties.

Above: Potato plants grown in tall containers make an attractive feature.

Opposite: For potato plants to thrive, grow them in a rich but light, well-drained soil and in a sunny position.

Sowing and transplanting

Potatoes are rarely grown from true seeds—it is possible, but true potato seeds are hard to find, and the whole process is slow and produces uncertain results. Instead, potatoes are grown from tubers called, confusingly, "seed potatoes." Don't try using store-bought potatoes because they are often sprayed with a chemical to prevent sprouting. Look for specially produced, certified disease-free seed potatoes from a garden center or mail-order supplier. Store the seed potatoes in a cool, light place if you are not ready to plant them right away.

You can plant small seed tubers whole, but cut large ones into smaller portions, which are referred to as seed pieces. Each piece must have at least two healthy buds (eyes). Cure cut seed pieces by storing them at 75°F (24°C) for one to two days.

Plant seed potatoes in early spring, digging individual planting holes deep enough to cover the tops of the tubers (or the sprouts, if you have sprouted them; see "Seeing Sprouts," opposite) with at least 1 inch (2.5cm) of soil. Space them 12 inches (30cm) apart in the row, with rows 15 inches (38cm) apart. Plant them about three or four weeks before the last frost is due in your area. Check with your local Cooperative Extension for suitable planting dates.

Potatoes are often affected by the fungus disease scab, which causes rough, brown, scabby patches on the skin. Because this disease likes alkaline conditions, potatoes will grow best in acidic soil. Do not add garden lime to the soil before planting potatoes.

Plants for pots

Early potatoes are ideal for growing in large containers that are at least 10 inches (25cm) across and 12 inches (30cm) deep. Or you can use special potato-planting kits, or even a garbage can, although you will need to add drainage holes.

Care

Protect early growth from frost by pulling soil right over the tops of the shoots or by laying floating row covers or even sheets of newspaper over them if frost is in the forecast.

Potato tubers normally form on underground stems, and the more of the plant that is under the soil, the larger the crop will be. As the plants grow, gradually cover more of the main stems with soil—either by mounding up the soil if

Seeing sprouts

For an extra-early crop, obtain seed potatoes as soon as they are available in winter, and place them in an egg carton or similar container, with the end of the tuber containing the most eyes facing up. Put them in a cool but brightly lit spot, such as a sunny windowsill in a cool room; short, sturdy, deep-green shoots will develop from the eyes. This process is known as sprouting and will give the potatoes a head start before you plant them outside later in the spring.

Potato continued

planted in the ground or by adding more potting mix if planted in containers. When mounding soil around the plants, draw it up on all sides of the main stems using a hoe. You will need to do this two or three times. In containers, add about 4 inches (10cm) of potting mix when the plants grow about 6 inches (15cm) tall, and continue adding potting mix in this way until the container is three-quarters full. Whether grown in the ground or in containers, always cover any exposed tubers. Parts that are exposed to light will turn green and poisonous, making those parts inedible.

Keep the soil evenly moist while the potato plants are growing. In dry conditions, many varieties produce tubers that fall apart when boiled.

Pest patrol

The black-and-yellow striped Colorado beetle is a serious pest of potatoes. Both adults and

Unwelcome fruit

Occasionally, potato plants produce small green fruit after they flower. These fruit look like unripe tomatoes—which is not surprising, because potatoes and tomatoes are closely related—but they should never be eaten. The fruit contain the toxic substance solanine. This is the same poisonous alkaloid found in another potato relative, deadly nightshade. Some varieties, such as 'Yukon Gold', have more of a tendency to produce fruit than others, and weather conditions may also have an effect.

If children will be around your potato plants, it is important that you remove and carefully discard any fruit that do form to prevent accidental poisoning.

Above: Flowers on a potato plant are a sign that tubers are ready for harvesting.

Right: A ridge will eventually form as the soil is mounded around the stems of the plants.

Opposite left: The best way to harvest the potatoes is to reach down into the soil and remove no more than two from each plant. Alternatively, pull up the whole plant to retrieve its complete crop

Opposite right: Consider growing less-common varieties, such as fingerling potatoes.

larvae feed voraciously on the leaves, and they are difficult to control. Use floating row covers from an early stage to help prevent infestations. Early varieties of potato are far less affected by the beetles than later varieties left to mature because the former have made much of their growth before the beetles arrive in force.

Time to pick

Start looking for potatoes as soon as the plants are flowering. You can harvest the first potatoes by carefully grabbling through the soil and pulling out a few of the largest tubers without disturbing the plant. The usual recommendation is to wait until the potatoes are the size of an egg, but impatient gardeners can sample them when they are a little smaller.

When most of the tubers are large enough, pull up the whole plant and sift through the soil with your fingers to unearth the crop. If you prefer, use a fork to lift the plants, but you will probably spear some potatoes on the prongs no matter how carefully you try to avoid it.

Good eating

Eat new potatoes as soon as possible after harvesting them. Wash the potatoes gently under running water. The delicate skins can usually be rubbed off with your thumb if you like, but most people prefer to eat new potatoes skins and all. However, remove any green skin—the rest of the potato will still be usable.

Simply boil the potatoes until they are just tender, and serve them with a sprinkling of salt, some melted butter, and freshly chopped parsley— the simpler the better to savor their wonderful taste.

Favorites

- **'Carola'** Heavy yielding, with oval tubers, pale-yellow skin and creamy-yellow flesh.
- **'Cranberry Red'** Rich-red skin and white flesh that is tinged with pink. Resistant to scab.
- **'Irish Cobbler'** Medium, round tubers with a distinctive flavor and creamy-white flesh.
- **'Red Norland'** Round or oval tubers with rosy-red skin and white flesh.
- **'Rose Finn Apple'** A waxy fingerling variety (named for its elongated tubers); good flavor.
- **'Superior'** Smooth, pink skin on round tubers.
- **'Yukon Gold'** Popular round tubers with pale yellow, flavorful flesh.
- **'Zolushka'** Medium oval tubers with smooth white skin and creamy-yellow flesh.

Scallion

Onions take time to develop their dense round bulbs, but you don't have to wait that long. Pull up scallions when the plants are just babies. Quick and easy to grow, they add mild onion flavor and crunch to both salads and cooked dishes.

The name game

Whether you call them "scallions" or "green onions"—or "salad onions," "spring onions," or "Welsh onions"—they are the same thing. They are all young onions pulled when they are about the thickness of a pencil with a length of white, blanched stem and a green top. These are often a variety of the bunching onion (*Allium fistulosum*), which is the name usually given in catalogs, or sometimes a cross between a bunching onion and a normal garden onion (*A. cepa*). You can also pull up any immature garden onions to use as scallions, but they will have a stronger flavor.

Sowing and transplanting

Sow the seeds thinly in furrows 9–12 inches (23–30cm) apart from early spring onward. Continue to sow small batches every 14 days for a supply throughout the summer.

Make a sowing in late summer or early fall to overwinter and provide a crop early the following spring.

Plants for pots

Scallions have shallow roots, so they will do well in containers. Simply sow the seeds thinly over the surface of the potting mix, and keep the mix moist.

Care

Keep the plants watered in dry spells. If you like a longer length of white stem, you can blanch them by pulling up a little soil around the sides of the plants. If you want to overwinter scallions, cover the rows with straw mulch, cloches, or floating row covers in severe, frosty weather.

Opposite: Scallions prefer a loose, rich soil, so consider adding compost to the soil before sowing. Make sure the soil stays moist while the plants are growing.

Time to pick

Most of the varieties selected for use as scallions remain straight and do not tend to form bulbs at the base. However, varieties that do form bulbous bases are also perfectly good to eat. Pull the scallions as soon as they reach a usable size, normally when the stems are about pencil thickness. Their flavor will intensify with age, so for a milder taste, pull up the scallions while the stems are still slender. Use a trowel to help uproot the plants to avoid breaking their tender stems.

Good eating

Scallions are simple to prepare. Just rinse and pull away the outer enfolding leaf to reveal the clean, pearly white center. Use scallions in salads or cooked dishes. When cooking scallions, add the green parts to the dish a little later than the white parts—the green parts take less time to cook. Some varieties have red stems, which add color to a salad.

Walk like an Egyptian

The perennial Egyptian onion, also called "the walking onion" or "tree onion," is popular with children. Instead of flowers, these onions produce groups of miniature bulbs at the tops of their stems. Once the bulblets grow large enough, their weight pulls the stem down to the ground, where the bulbs can take root and grow. In this way, the plants will eventually "walk" right across your vegetable plot. Both the bulblets and the leaves are edible.

Favorites

- **'Crimson Forest'** Deep-red stems becoming pink as outer leaves are removed. Sweet and mild. A little slower growing than white scallions.
- **'Evergreen Hardy'** Overwinters even in cold areas. Forms clusters of stems.
- **'Guardsman'** A cross between *Allium cepa* and *A. fistulosum,* this quick, early scallion has strong growth and a good flavor.
- **'Ishikura'** Has long, slender stems, deep-green leaves, and tender, mildly pungent flavor.
- **'Mini Purplette'** Early scallion with purple-tinged stems. You can let it continue to grow to form small pearl onions.
- **'Parade'** Straight, nonbulbing stems; vigorous, uniform grower.
- **'Tokyo Long White'** Scallion with a pungent flavor and long stems.
- **'White Lisbon'** Popular, quick-growing scallion with straight stems and a mild flavor.
- **'White Spear'** Scallion ideal for hot regions.

Spinach

There may be confusion about the iron content in spinach, but it is a wonderfully healthy food—packed with vitamins and minerals. If you have childhood memories of soggy, bitter, overcooked green sludge, you will be happy to find that home-grown spinach is absolutely delicious.

Above: Young spinach leaves are mild enough for a salad; however, you can also harvest them for cooking.

Opposite: When harvesting large, mature leaves on a cut-and-come-again basis, a sharp knife or kitchen scissors can be handy to avoid tugging out the whole plant.

Sowing and transplanting

Spinach is sensitive to the length of the day and will often go to seed when there are 13 hours or more of daylight, particularly if this is associated with warm weather and dry soil. Start sowing seeds in early spring, choosing bolt-resistant varieties, and continue to sow batches every three weeks or so. Afternoon shade can help sowings made in hot regions. Seeds sown after the longest day of the year should not bolt, and you can keep the harvesting continuing well into fall by covering the plants with cloches or floating row covers. Sow the seeds thinly in rows about 12 inches (30cm) apart.

Care

Thin the seedlings in stages to approximately 6 inches (15cm) apart, using the thinnings as salad greens. Overcrowded plants are more likely to bolt, so thin spinach plants at an early stage. Keep the soil thoroughly moist at all times, especially in hot weather. Summer-sown plants will crop for longer if you give them an occasional high-nitrogen liquid fertilizer. Protect with floating row covers if insects, such as aphids, flea beetles, leafhoppers, or leaf miners, are a problem.

Time to pick

Harvest the leaves as soon as they are large enough, using the youngest for salads. As soon as one or two plants start to show signs of bolting, harvest the entire row and sow again. You can harvest later-sown plants on a cut-and-come-again basis by picking individual leaves from

Popeye's favorite veg

Most people remember Popeye promoting healthy, iron-rich spinach—and they have also heard that the high-iron content claimed for spinach was the result of an error with a decimal point, so it had less iron than first stated. The latter is a myth. Spinach has high levels of iron, as well as other vitamins and minerals, such as beta carotene, vitamin C, vitamin K, calcium, folate, lutein, magnesium, and potassium, making spinach a nutritious vegetable. However, it also has high levels of oxalic acid, which prevents the body from absorbing some nutrients in spinach. Some studies report that fast-growing spinach cultivars have lower levels of oxalic acid.

the outsides of the plants. Spinach shrinks considerably during cooking, so pick much more than you think you will need.

Good eating

Wash the leaves well under running water, particularly the varieties with wrinkled leaves because these can trap soil. Shake them dry, or give them a quick turn in a salad spinner to get rid of most of the moisture. Cook the leaves in a saucepan with no added water, turning them frequently until they have collapsed and are tender but are still bright green—do not overcook. Squeeze well to drain off any water before serving or adding to a dish, such as pasta or a casserole. Spinach also cooks well in a microwave.

Favorites

- **'Bloomsdale Long Standing'** A bolt-resistant spinach with thick, textured, tasty leaves.
- **'Emu'** Smooth, mid-green leaves, slow to bolt.
- **'Harmony Hybrid'** Intensely ruffled, deep-green leaves, early to crop and slow to bolt.
- **'Melody'** Hardy and vigorous, with mid-green, tasty leaves.
- **'Razzle Dazzle'** One of the fastest growers, with pointed, arrowhead-shaped leaves. High yielding.
- **'Renegade'** Quick to crop, with smooth, light-green leaves.
- **'Space'** Quick growing, with large, smooth leaves of good flavor. Slow to bolt.
- **'Tyee'** Upright growth means less soil splashes on the deeply crinkled leaves. Vigorous and bolt resistant.
- **'7-Green'** Quick to crop and high yielding, with mild flavor and medium-green leaves.

Swiss chard

This is a vegetable that deserves to be more widely grown. The quilted green leaves taste similar to spinach, but the plants are easier to grow, being far less likely to bolt. The thick leaf midribs are also tasty, producing two vegetables for the price of one. As a final bonus, the colorful red-, yellow-, or white-stemmed varieties are highly decorative, making them an attractive addition to any garden.

Perpetual spinach

Swiss chard has striking, thick, often brightly colored leaf stems, but perpetual spinach, or leaf beet, has many more slender, green stems and is cultivated for its leaves only. Grow it in the same way as Swiss chard, but space the plants more closely together at 4–6 inches (10–15cm) apart.

Sowing and transplanting

Sow the seeds from midspring to late summer in a sunny spot in reasonably fertile, moisture-retentive soil. In hot regions, you can sow seeds in partial shade.

Although Swiss chard may look like spinach, it is related to beet, and it has similar seed clusters that produce more than one seedling. (See "Beet," pages 108–109.) Space the seeds about 3 inches (7.5cm) apart in rows 18 inches (45cm) apart.

Care

Thin the seedlings in stages to 6–8 inches (15–20cm) apart. You can use the thinnings as salad greens. Keep the soil moist at all times, especially in hot weather. Provide an occasional high-nitrogen liquid fertilizer as the season progresses.

You can overwinter summer-sown plants, which will produce an early spring crop. In cold areas, use floating row covers to provide protection against severe frost.

Above: A raindrop of colors will make Swiss chard leaves and stems attractive both in the garden and on the dinner table.

Time to pick

Start to pick leaves from the outside of the plants as soon as they are large enough, using a sharp knife to cut the stems at the base. Harvest regularly to encourage the plants to continue producing fresh growth. Old, overly large leaves become somewhat coarse and are not as good to eat, so try to pick them young. Overwintered plants will eventually bolt to seed in the spring—discard them at that point.

Good eating

Separate the leaf blades from the stems and midribs—the stems require slightly longer

Favorites

- **'Bright Lights'** Red, yellow, orange, pink, and white stems feature in this colorful mix.
- **'Eldorado'** Deep-gold stems and dark green leaves on hardy plants. With a little protection, they will continue to provide a crop throughout the winter.
- **'Fordhook Giant'** A well-established Swiss chard, with dark-green, quilted leaves and wide, creamy-white midribs. Tolerant of both cold and heat.
- **'Golden Sunrise'** Deep-gold stems and veins; the color is well developed even on young leaves. Excellent as a baby leaf as well as full size.
- **'Lucullus'** Similar to 'Fordhook Giant' but slightly faster to crop. Heavy yielding.
- **'Magenta Sunset'** Purple-red leaf stalks and midribs and dark, glossy leaves make this an eye-catching plant.
- **'Neon Lights'** A combination of distinct, bright stem colors—gold, red, white, and rich magenta, with bright-green leaf blades.
- **'Ruby Red'** Sometimes called "rhubarb Swiss chard" because the crimson stems make it look similar to rhubarb. Heavily crinkled, deep green leaves and a mild flavor.

Above: Start cutting the leaves of Swiss chard from the outside of the plant as you need them, using a sharp knife.

cooking than the leaves. Wash the stems, and rinse the leaves well. Although they are usually deeply quilted, they do not seem to hold the dirt as much as spinach leaves, so grittiness is not such a problem.

Cook the leaves in the same way as spinach. They are more robust in texture and perhaps not so finely flavored, but they are still tasty. You can chop the stems (or leave them whole if not too large), and steam or lightly boil them until just tender. Mix the cooked stems and cooked greens together with a pat of butter and a grating of fresh nutmeg, or serve them as separate vegetables. Swiss chard is particularly good served au gratin—covered with a cheese sauce, sprinkled with grated cheese and bread crumbs, and browned in the oven.

Blueberry page 140

Herbs page 142

Favorite herbs page 144

Pepper and chili page 150

Strawberry page 154

Tomato page 156

Zucchini and other summer squash page 160

Low-maintenance vegetables page 164

Worth
the wait

These fruits and vegetables may not be the fastest to produce a crop, but they are still worth growing. Many of them make up for their longer growing time by being particularly easy to grow, so they need less of your attention to care for them. Others produce an abundant harvest or have some other special attribute that has earned them their place in your garden.

Blueberry

With attractive nodding, creamy flowers and stunning fall leaf color to add to their delicious, dusky blue fruit, blueberries are well worth a place in your garden. These plants are a little particular about soil, but this won't be a problem—they are a perfect crop for growing in containers.

Plants for pots

Use a large container, at last 12 inches (30cm) across, and make sure it has plenty of drainage holes. Fill it with ericaceous potting mix (this is the type sold for rhododendrons, azaleas, and camellias). You can add some shredded bark or bark chips to the potting mix with if you like; the mix should be light and free draining but moisture retentive. Adding some sulfur granules will help to keep the pH stable over time. Set the blueberry plant in the center of the pot, and firm it in well. Water the plant, and finally cover the surface of the mix with some bark to help retain the moisture.

Sowing and transplanting

Blueberries need acidic soil without a trace of lime. Test your soil with a pH kit if you want to grow the bushes in the ground. The pH should be no higher than 4–5. In theory, you can amend alkaline soil by adding sulfur, but it is difficult to adjust the soil correctly. If you don't have the right soil in your patch (and many gardens may not), it is much easier to grow plants in containers of suitable lime-free potting mix.

Whether you grow blueberry plants in the ground or in pots, purchase well-established, container-grown plants from a garden center or nursery. Although many blueberry plants are self-pollinating, you will get a much better crop if two or more different types are planted to pollinate each other.

Which blueberry?

There are three main types of blueberry, and which one you grow will depend on where you live. In Zones 3–7, northern highbush blueberries are recommended. These require winter temperatures of below 45°F (7°C). In warm areas, you can grow rabbiteye (Zones 6–9) and southern highbush types (Zones 6–10). These are more tolerant of heat and dry conditions, and they don't require as much winter chill to form their fruit buds.

Favorites

Northern highbush

- **'Blue Crop'** Midseason, with large, flavorful berries. More drought resistant than some types.
- **'Duke'** Early season, good yields of medium to large, sweet, mildly flavored fruit.
- **'Patriot'** Early season. Upright growth with large, sweet fruit. Good fall color.

Rabbiteye

- **'Centurion'** Mid- to late season, with medium to large, deep-blue, good-quality fruit.
- **'Premier'** Early to midseason, with large, light-blue, favorful fruit. Heavy cropping.
- **'Tifblue'** Midseason, light-blue, tasty berries. Excellent fall leaf color, making this an ornamental choice.

Southern highbush

- **'Misty'** Early to midseason, with medium to large blue fruit. A good companion for 'Sharpblue'.
- **'Sharpblue'** Early and vigorous, with tasty, medium berries. Good for areas with mild winters.
- **'Sunshine Blue'** A compact plant ideal for containers. Midseason, with small, flavorful berries.

Pest patrol

Birds love blueberries, and they are not fussy about waiting until the fruit is ripe. As soon as the berries start to swell, cover your plants with netting to keep marauders at bay, or you may find your bushes stripped.

Care

Keep blueberries well watered; they are shallow-rooting, thirsty plants. If you live in an area with hard water, use rainwater.

Feed with an ericaceous fertilizer throughout the growing season. (Follow the package directions regarding how often to apply it.)

Berries are carried on shoots produced in previous years. In winter or early spring, cut down one or two of the oldest, least productive branches to soil level to encourage strong, healthy replacement shoots.

Time to pick

Berries turn from green to blue-black, with a dusty bloom. The best time to pick the fruit is three or four days after they turn completely black because they become much sweeter in those few days. Pull the berries gently; if they are ripe, they will come away easily.

Opposite left: After flowering, young green berries will appear in clusters on older shoots.

Opposite top: Once a dusty bloom appears on the berries, inspect them regularly for harvesting. The darkest berries will be the sweetest.

Above: At the end of the season as the leaves begin to turn color, it will be obvious which are old and which are new shoots.

Herbs

There are so many flavorful culinary herbs that the main problem is usually finding enough space to grow as many different types as you would like. Most are easy to cultivate, making them ideal for the busy gardener.

Above: A window box full of herbs can also be an ornamental feature on a patio or in a courtyard. You can move herbs grown in a container to a more sheltered position as the seasons change so that you can extend the picking season.

The major value of culinary herbs is their ability to flavor food, but many herb plants are also decorative and earn a place in any garden on that count alone. They make an attractive feature when grouped together and grown in a small, formal herb garden, but they're just as much at home dotted among flowers or vegetables or growing in containers. They have a good range of leaf colors, shapes, and forms, and some types also have attractive flowers.

Where to grow herbs

Most herbs like an open, sunny position, and their flavor is usually better when they are grown in free-draining soil that is low in nutrients. In rich soil, they will make plenty of lush growth, but that growth will not be as aromatic as plants grown in poor soil.

The fragrant oils in herbs' leaves and stems are released when the plant is lightly crushed or bruised—pinching scented leaves as you pass by is almost irresistible. If you plant herbs near a walkway where their growth will be brushed as you pass or in gaps in paths where they will be trodden underfoot, you will release delicious, uplifting fragrances as you walk past.

Plant herbs that you are growing to use in cooking near the kitchen door to make harvesting the leaves more practical. Those sprigs of thyme and parsley somehow don't look like such essential ingredients when gathering them involves a trek to the far end of the yard on a cold, rainy evening, so be sure they are always close at hand. In the winter months, have some pots of the herbs you like best growing on a sunny windowsill in the house.

Plants for pots

Many herbs are perfect for containers, even window boxes and hanging baskets. They don't demand rich soil or frequent feeding and can usually cope with fairly dry conditions, so they won't need the twice-daily watering that many vegetables might require, especially in hot areas.

Good drainage is vital for herbs, so be sure your container has sufficient drainage holes and a good thick layer of coarse material (such as broken clay pieces, pebbles, or chunky gravel) at the bottom. If necessary, set the container on pot feet or pieces of wood or brick to raise it off the ground so that the water can drain away. Fill the container with a good-quality potting mix.

Growing plants in containers is particularly useful for rampant herbs, such as mint, which can take over the garden if their spreading roots are given free access to soil in a garden bed.

Planting a **window box**

1. After preparing the window box with the drainage material and potting mix, place the herbs how you would like them on top of the soil. Make sure they have the growing space indicated on the plant labels. Make a planting hole at one end.

2. With the first herb plant centered in the planting hole, fill the gaps in the hole with the potting mix, making sure the root-ball is covered and firming down the mix around the plant.

3. Continue planting the window box with the other herbs in the same way. Make sure you handle the plants carefully, supporting the stems on both sides at the soil level as you remove them from the pot.

4. Water in the plants, and make sure the mix stays slightly moist for the first couple of weeks while the plants become established.

Year-round supplies

A few herbs are evergreen, but most don't supply much growth to harvest in the colder winter months. In addition to keeping a few pots on the windowsill for using fresh, make the most of the summer bounty by drying and freezing herbs for winter use. Hang up loose bunches of freshly picked shoots in a dry, airy place, or use the microwave—lay sprigs between two sheets of paper towel, and microwave them on full power for a couple of minutes or until they are dry and brittle.

Freezing preserves an almost fresh flavor. Chop the herbs finely; pack them in ice-cube trays; fill up with water; and freeze. To use, drop the herb ice cubes into dishes, such as soups, stews, and casseroles, as you are cooking them.

Favorite herbs

With so many herbs from which to choose, the toughest part can be deciding what to grow. Some of these herbs are easy to grow from seeds; others are best bought as young plants, especially if you are impatient to start sampling their delights.

Basil

Chives

A perennial herb, chives form a clump of deep green, hollow, spearlike leaves that have a delicate onion flavor. The pretty, papery, lilac flowers are edible, too. Sow chives in spring in pots indoors, and plant outside when large enough in an open, sunny position. Divide and replant the clumps every two or three years to keep them vigorous. Named types of chives are hard to find, but specialty herb nurseries do have some, such as 'Grolau', 'Forescate', and 'Profusion'. 'Purly' and 'Staro' are available to grow from seeds. Garlic (or Chinese) chives have flat leaves, white flowers, and a stronger flavor.

Time to pick: Cut the leaves at the base as required, and chop finely before using. Chives can be dried, but they are probably best frozen.

Basil

This tender annual has a wonderful warm, clovelike aroma and is a perfect partner for tomatoes, but it can be used in many other dishes, too. Sow the seeds indoors in midspring, and harden off the seedlings thoroughly before planting them outside once all risk of frost is over. Choose a warm, sheltered spot in full sun. Pinch off the growing tips frequently to keep the plants bushy. There are dozens of different types of basil to try, including purple-leaved kinds, such as 'Amethyst Improved' and 'Purple Ruffles'; those with hints of different flavors, such as cinnamon, lime, and lemon; and those with different shapes and sizes of leaves, such as serrated 'Spicy Saber', huge 'Lettuce Leaf', and tiny 'Green Bouquet'.

Time to pick: Best used fresh, straight after picking. It is difficult to store, but steeping the leaves in olive oil will impart their distinctive aroma to the oil.

Chives

Coriander

The strong, refreshing flavor of cilantro leaves from the annual coriander plant has become popular in recent years. Both the lobed cilantro leaves and the coriander seeds are used in cooking, and the leaves are a good choice for a microgreen. (See "Microgreens," page 99.) The leaves look somewhat like those of flat-leaf parsley, which is a close relative. Sow coriander seeds from early spring to midsummer where it will grow; keep the seedlings moist, or the plants may bolt to seed prematurely. The plant will grow in light shade as well as sun. 'Santo' is a slow-bolting selection.

Time to pick: Pick the leaves as required, and use as soon as possible after picking. Place bunches of the dry, ripe seed heads upside down in a paper bag to catch the citrus-flavor seeds.

Dill

Coriander

Dill

The feathery, threadlike leaves of dill make it a decorative herb, and the aniseed flavor goes well with fish. It is an annual, and you should sow it where it will grow from early to midspring. Make successional sowings every two or three weeks. Unlike many herbs, dill prefers a fairly moist, fertile soil, and it may bolt if it is too dry or the roots are disturbed.

Time to pick: Cut the leaves as required; once the flowers appear, cut the plant back hard to promote fresh leafy growth. You can use the seeds in cooking; cut the seed heads, and place them in a paper bag to catch the seeds. If you leave the seed heads on the plant too long, they will self-sow and can become a nuisance.

Fennel

It is similar to dill, but fennel has even more fine, threadlike foliage and a stronger licorice flavor. Fennel is a hardy perennial that can be sown indoors in early spring or directly in the ground where it will grow in midspring. It likes an open, sunny position, and because it is tall at 3–6 feet (1–2m), it makes a good plant for the back of a bed or border. It self-seeds prodigiously, so remove the flowers if you do not want to harvest the seeds (which can also be used in cooking). Bronze fennel has dramatic purple foliage.

Time to pick: Snip off the feathery leaves as soon as they are large enough. They are best eaten fresh, although you can use them dried or frozen. Both unripe and ripe seeds are good for flavoring a range of dishes.

Oregano

Fennel

Marjoram and oregano

A neat, low-growing plant, sweet marjoram is usually grown as an annual and has small, delicately aromatic leaves. It is closely related to oregano, which is taller and shrubbier, grown as a perennial, and has a pungent but somewhat less refined aroma. Both plants like a reasonably fertile soil and a position in full sun. Pinch off the shoot tips frequently to encourage bushy growth, and clip the plants back when they start flowering.

Time to pick: Pinch young shoots as required. These herbs dry well, retaining much of their flavor; they can also be frozen.

Mint

Summer savory

This annual herb, with its warmly fragrant leaves, is not as widely known as it deserves to be. Savory adds a rich aroma to many dishes, especially beans—in parts of Europe it is known as the "bean herb." It likes a well-drained soil and a warm, sunny spot. In midspring, sow it in the ground where it will grow. To encourage the production of fresh leaves, cut the plants back when flowering starts, although you may want to leave some plants to bloom because the whorls of pink flowers are attractive to bees. Its relative winter savory is a shrubby hardy perennial with a less refined flavor.

Time to pick: Cut sprigs to use as required. Savory dries and freezes well.

Mint

The fresh tang of mint has plenty of uses in the kitchen. Perennial mint is ideally suited to growing in containers because the spreading, invasive roots can become a nuisance in an open bed. It is easier to start mint with a section of root from a friend or neighbor; bury it 2 inches (5cm) deep. You can also find a good supply of named types of mint at herb nurseries. These are available in a wide range of flavors and leaf colors. Among the best are: 'Apple Mint', with large, soft leaves; 'Curly', a crinkled-leaf type with a spearmint flavor; and 'Ginger', with sweetly fragrant, golden-variegated leaves. There are also Eau-de-Cologne mint, pineapple mint, spearmint, peppermint, and orange mint, among others.

Time to pick: Snip the young shoots as soon as they start to appear aboveground in spring. For winter use, either plant a section of root in a pot and let it grow in a warm place indoors or dry or freeze leaves in summer.

Summer Savory

Tarragon

Thyme

A particularly useful herb with a delightfully warm, peppery aroma, thyme comes in many forms. Common thyme makes a spreading, low-growing plant with small, aromatic leaves. In summer, it bears masses of pretty flowers in shades of white and pink, which are often smothered in bees. Plant in an open, sunny, well-drained position. You can cut it back hard after flowering, and it will soon produce leafy regrowth. There are literally dozens of different species and varieties of thyme, some upright and bushy, some low and creeping. Many of them are decorative, with variegated leaves and colorful blooms. Look for 'Golden King', 'Silver Posie', 'Porlock', 'Annie Hall', 'Citriodorus', and 'Doone Valley'.

Time to pick: Pick leafy sprigs as required. Small-leaved thyme dries well, retaining a strong flavor.

Tarragon

One of the most prized herbs for cooking, tarragon has strongly aromatic foliage with a warm aniseed fragrance. It is particularly good with chicken dishes. French tarragon is the best type for culinary use; Russian tarragon is easier to grow and decorative, but it lacks flavor. French tarragon does not usually set viable seeds, so you will have to seek out plants from a reliable supplier. Plant them in a sheltered, warm, sunny position in free-draining soil. In cold areas, some winter protection with cloches or floating row covers may be necessary. Alternatively, you can root cuttings in the summer and overwinter them under cover.

Time to pick: Collect shoots as required, but let the young plants of French tarragon become well established before snipping. The leaves are best used fresh, but you can freeze or dry them.

Thyme

Pepper and chili

With their wide range of colors and shapes, peppers can be ornamental as well as productive, and they make first-rate container plants. From juicy, sweet peppers to searingly hot chilies, there are peppers to suit all tastes.

Sowing and transplanting

Peppers do best if you sow them early in spring in a greenhouse or in a propagator on a sunny windowsill, which will give them a reasonably long growing season. Alternatively, buy young plants from a garden center later in the spring. The advantage of raising your own plants from seeds is that you will have a much greater choice of varieties.

Replant the seedlings when they are large enough to be handled, and pot the young plants individually in separate containers. Harden off thoroughly before planting them outside in a sheltered position in early summer.

Plants for pots

Peppers do well in a container on a sunny patio; the size of the container required depends on the variety of pepper because some plants are far more compact than others. Mix some water-retaining granules with the potting mix for containers to reduce the risk of the plants drying out.

Care

Use stakes or a cage to support the plants as they grow. If the weather turns cool, use cloches or floating row covers to give them a little extra protection. Once flowering begins,

Above: Once pepper plants begin to flower, providing a potassium-base fertilizer will help the plant to concentrate on producing fruit.

Right: Pepper plants are a good choice for growing in containers, but be sure they have adequate support. Here, stakes attached to a wooden crate ensure that the supports don't fall over.

give the plants a high-potassium liquid fertilizer regularly. (Tomato fertilizer is ideal.) Keep the soil moist at all times because drying out can lead to blossom end rot—a brown, sunken area on the end of the pepper opposite the stalk. The damage is done while the fruit is forming, but it does not show up until later.

Time to pick

You can harvest sweet peppers as soon as they are large enough to use, while still green. The flavor at this stage will not be as sweet as when the fruit is ripe. However, picking the earliest-forming peppers before they ripen will produce a much bigger overall harvest because the plants will be stimulated to produce a larger crop. If you pick later peppers when they start to show the first signs of changing color, they will continue to ripen after being harvested. Use pruners to cut the stems because they are tough.

Like sweet peppers, you can harvest chilies at different stages of maturity. The riper the chili, the hotter it is. Traditionally, long, slender chilies, such as 'Cayenne', are braided together in a rope known as a ristra, which is hung in an airy place indoors. This keeps the chilies handy for use through the fall and winter, and is decorative, too. Use only perfect chilies, and check the ristra frequently to remove any that start to rot.

Good eating

The part of the chili that contains the most heat is the membrane that holds the seeds. If you like your chili flavor with less heat, remove and discard all the seeds and all the white membrane that surrounds them.

Taming the burn

Peppers contain a substance called capsaicin, which is what gives chilies their heat. It is an irritant substance that produces a burning sensation when it comes into contact with sensitive areas of skin or mucous membranes. Different types of peppers contain different amounts of capsaicin. Their heat is measured in Scoville units, with sweet peppers rated at 0, while the hottest chilies (such as habanero) can reach a mind-blowing 1 million units.

Mild to moderate chili heat can produce pleasant and even euphoric sensations in some people, but strong chilies must be handled with care. Be particularly careful not to touch your eyes after handling them because this can cause intense pain; the mouth, lips, and throat can also be badly affected. (Pepper sprays used for self-defense and riot control contain capsaicin, which gives you an idea of its power.) If you overdo it when eating hot chilies, drinking water will not help, but milk or yogurt will take some of the heat out of the situation.

Types of peppers and chilies

Available in a range of shapes and colors, sweet peppers can be eaten raw or used cooked. The blocky shape of bell peppers makes them popular for stuffing, but other shapes are available, too.

Smaller than sweet peppers, chilies are more fiery in flavor. They range from mild types to searingly hot ones that should be used with caution. The heat often depends on the weather and growing conditions as much as the variety. If you are not sure how hot a chili is, lightly touch a cut surface near the chili's tip with your tongue before adding it to a dish.

Favorites
Sweet bell peppers

- **'Ace'** An early, high-yielding F1 hybrid with a good crop. Grows well in cooler areas.
- **'Baby Belle'** Tiny peppers about 2 inches (5cm) tall, packed with sweet flavor. Quick to ripen to bright red.
- **'Blushing Beauty'** This pepper starts off ivory cream instead of green, then turns peach and orange to scarlet as it ripens. It makes a beautiful ornamental plant because there are usually several different colors on it at one time.
- **'California Wonder'** Sturdy upright plants with peppers that have thick flesh with a mild, sweet flavor.
- **'Golden California Wonder'** has a bright-gold color that ripens to orange-red.
- **'Chocolate Beauty'** Smooth, medium peppers that turn an unusual reddish chocolate-brown when ripe. Very sweet flavor.
- **'Early Sunsation'** Heavy yielding, with large peppers that ripen to bright yellow. Stays crisp and sweet.
- **'Purple Star'** Deep purple, glossy peppers on compact plants. Early to crop.
- **'Redskin'** Early cropping, with plenty of peppers ripening to a glowing red. Its compact, cascading habit makes it ideal for containers and small spaces.

- **'Yum Yum Gold'** Miniature peppers ripening to orange and gold. Heavy yielding.

Other sweet peppers

- **'Biscayne'** Long, ribbed, cylindrical fruit, pale green ripening to red. An F1 hybrid variety.
- **'Corno di Toro'** The name means "bull's horn," which describes the long, gently curving shape well. Sweet flavor. There are red and yellow selections.
- **'Lipstick'** The long, tapering peppers are dark green, ripening to a rich red. Grows well in cool areas.
- **'Sweet Banana'** Long, slender, pointy, yellow peppers ripen to red. As the name implies, sweet tasting.

Chilies

- **'Anaheim'** Normally used green, but the long pods ripen to red. Productive. Mild to medium heat.
- **'Cayenne'** A compact-growing bush with long, slim, twisted peppers. Very hot.
- **'Conchos'** A Jalapeño-type pepper used in Mexican cooking. Cylindrical, dark-green to scarlet peppers. Medium to hot.
- **'Explosive Ember'** Compact plants with striking purple foliage. Small, tapered serrano-type peppers ripen from purple through yellow to red, and form early in the season. Excellent for containers. Hot.
- **'Hungarian Hot Wax'** Smooth, tapering peppers ripen from yellow to red and orange. Medium hot.
- **'Kung Pao Hybrid'** Tall plants carry an abundance of long, thin, curved peppers. Very hot.
- **'Red Mushroom'** Oddly shaped, wrinkled peppers with a cap that makes them look like a mushroom or hat. Habanero type. Very hot.
- **'Scotch Bonnet'** Oval peppers, similar to habanero peppers. They have a fruity flavor beneath the intense spiciness. Very hot.
- **'Super Chile Hybrid'** Peppers ripen from green to yellow to red, and point upward, above the foliage on compact plants, making them decorative. Hot.
- **'Zavory'** Habanero peppers such as this are usually very hot, but 'Zavory' is a mild variety that allows the distinctive fruity flavor to come through. Plenty of firm, blocky peppers. Mild.

Bell pepper

'Cayenne' chili

'Scotch Bonnet' chili

'Sweet Banana' pepper

Strawberry

Nothing beats the flavor of a ripe, sun-basked strawberry eaten straight from the plant. With the new types and growing methods, you can now grow strawberries as annuals, instead of following the traditional method that required you to wait.

Below: Strawberries are easy to grow in window boxes and other containers. Use a not-too-rich potting mix, and water regularly once flowering starts.

Opposite: Freshly picked, ripe strawberries have a flavor far superior than any store-bought strawberries, which often makes them a first choice, even where gardening space is at a premium.

Which strawberries to choose?

There are two types of strawberries to grow as annuals: the June bearers, which carry a single, heavy crop of large, juicy fruit in early to midsummer, and the everbearing types. Everbearers produce crops in two or three flushes between late spring and fall. The best everbearers to grow as an annual crop are the day-neutral types. These produce fruit through the summer until the first frost. The fruit is small, but they make up for this in productivity and speed and ease of cropping.

Favorites

Day-neutral types

- **'Albion'** Firm, conical fruit with an excellent flavor.
- **'Eversweet'** Good crops of flavorful berries. Recommended for hot and humid zones, where other types might struggle.
- **'Seascape'** A popular strawberry with relatively large, deep-red berries.
- **'Tribute'** One of the earliest day-neutral types, with firm, sweet berries. A good late-summer and fall crop.
- **'Tristar'** Tasty small to medium fruit. Good in hanging baskets.

Sowing and transplanting

Strawberries are perennial plants, but by treating them as annuals, you can enjoy much quicker crops. This growing method is also more suitable in either cool or warm regions.

Plant strawberry plants in early to midspring in free-draining, moisture-retentive soil. In hot southern areas, plant in early fall. When planting in a bed, make rows of mounds about 8 inches (20cm) high and set the plants in the mounds 12 inches (30cm) apart. Make sure that the crown of the plant is just level with the soil.

Plants in pots

Strawberries grow well in containers. The fruit will be kept clean, away from ground soil and pests, and will be less likely to rot in damp conditions than if grown in the ground. Special strawberry pots, with multiple planting holes, are attractive and make good use of a small space, but you can use other pots—even window boxes and hanging baskets—just as successfully.

Care

Remove any flowers on the newly planted strawberries until the end of June; then let them set fruit. Day-neutral types produce

Quick and easy strawberry jam

This freezer jam has a softer set than normal, but it retains a really delicious, fresh strawberry flavor. Different brands of pectin have different quantities and instructions; always check the package.

Ingredients
4 cups mashed strawberries
1½ cups sugar
1 package freezer jam pectin

In a large bowl, crush the strawberries using a vegetable masher. Add the sugar, and stir well until dissolved; then stir in the pectin. Ladle into small, freezer-safe jars or plastic containers (leaving a small gap at the top for the mixture to expand on freezing), and seal. Let stand in a warm place for 30 minutes before freezing. Remove from the freezer as required. Once thawed, keep the jam refrigerated.

fewer runners than June-bearing strawberries, but pinch off the runners that appear so that all the plants' energy goes into producing fruit.

Give a dressing of a balanced fertilizer in midsummer, and water the plants in dry spells as soon as flowering starts—this will help to increase fruit size. Mulching around plants planted in the ground with straw will help to keep the soil moist and protect the fruit from pests and soil splashes. Once fruiting has finished or the first frost arrives, pull up the plants.

Pest patrol

Birds love strawberries and won't wait until they are ripe. Where birds are a problem, cover the plants with netting as soon as the fruit starts to show color.

Time to pick

Pick strawberries as soon as they have full color, breaking the stem so that the calyx (the green outer whorl) remains on the fruit. Eat the berries as soon as possible after picking. If they won't be eaten right away, store strawberries in a cool place; however, do not refrigerate them, because doing so will ruin the flavor.

Tomato

Even if you have room for only a hanging basket, there's a tomato type for you. Freshly picked, completely ripe tomatoes have a wonderful taste and aroma that fruit from the grocery store can never achieve.

Sowing and transplanting

Tomatoes love warmth. Sow seeds indoors from about four weeks before the last frost is due, and place them in a warm spot at 70–85°F (21–30°C) to germinate. Once most of the seeds have germinated, move the seedlings to a light but still warm position. When they are large enough to handle, transplant the seedlings into individual pots. Harden them off thoroughly when all danger of frost is past, and plant them in the ground in a warm, sheltered, sunny position. Planting distances will depend on the variety, so check the seed packet. Tomatoes like good, nutrient-rich soil, so add some well-rotted garden compost to the bottom of the planting hole if you can.

If you don't have a suitable environment to raise your own seeds, young plants are readily available at garden centers from late spring onward, although you won't have as much choice of the variety when buying.

Above: Once there is no longer a danger of frost in your area, you can plant young tomato plants outdoors in a sunny, sheltered position.

Above right: For the best sweet, juicy cherry tomatoes in a hanging basket, look for varieties that have been especially developed to grow in them.

Plants for pots

Tomatoes are a good candidate for growing in a container filled with a rich potting mix. Bush tomatoes, especially those that produce small tomatoes, such as cherry tomatoes, are a good choice for hanging baskets. You can even grow indeterminate types in a large 3-gallon (11L) container or a bag of soil mix and train them up a stake or other support. (See "Growing in a Bag," page 46, and "Supporting Roles," pages 56–57.)

Upside-down planters

A novel and space-saving way to grow tomatoes is in a plastic "upside-down" planter. You set the tomato so that it emerges through a hole in the bottom of the planter; then you fill the planter with soil and hang it up like a hanging basket. Some types let you grow other plants, such as herbs or lettuce, on top. The advantages are that no stakes or supports are needed for the tomato plants; they are kept away from soil pests; and the tomatoes are easy to pick. However, like a hanging basket, the planter can be awkward to reach for watering. Because it will be heavy, make sure the support is securely attached.

Tomato **habits**

Different types of tomatoes have different growing habits. The easiest to grow are bush (determinate) types, which make compact, bushy plants. They usually have one main flush of fruit, although some varieties continue to produce a crop for longer periods. Bush types are the best type of tomato to grow if you have little space and time.

Indeterminate (also called cordon or vine) types make long, sprawling stems that continue growing and flowering until stopped by frost, so they have a longer season of producing a crop. They need more support than bush types, and you usually need to remove their sideshoots regularly to keep the plants under control. Some gardeners prefer the flavor of indeterminate tomatoes; however, there are now plenty of bush types from which to choose that produce sweet, flavorful tomatoes.

Care

If the weather turns cold after planting the tomatoes outside, protect the plants with cloches until the weather warms up. You can support bush tomatoes with either a stake or tomato cage. However, for indeterminate tomatoes, use a stake because a cage can make it difficult to remove the sideshoots. Tie the stems loosely to their supports with a soft material at regular intervals.

Once flowering starts, begin feeding the plants with a high-potassium liquid fertilizer. Do not feed the plants earlier than this, or you will get large, lush, leafy plants that are slower to flower and produce fruit.

Regular watering is important, especially once the plants start to flower. Keep the growing medium moist at all times. If you are growing tomatoes in containers, it is a good idea to mix in some moisture-retaining granules at planting time.

Left: A plastic pole or wooden stake is a good option for supporting vinelike indeterminate tomatoes. As the plant grows, tie it loosely to the support using a piece of garden string, plant ties, or even strips of cloth.

Tomato continued

netting. Make sure the trusses of tomatoes are supported so that they do not lie on the ground, where they may rot or be attacked by slugs.

Time to pick

Pick the tomatoes when they develop their full color. You can pick them as soon as they start to show color because they will continue to ripen off the plant, but their best flavor develops when they ripen fully "on the vine."

All shapes and sizes

Tomatoes are not just red and round. Their colors when fully ripe range from green to yellow, peach, orange, pink, scarlet, purple, chocolate brown, and almost black. There are even white types, and some that are striped or multicolored.

Tomatoes can be any size from tiny grape to huge 2 pounders (1kg). As far as shapes go, there are cherry, pear, plum, banana, smoothly spherical, deeply ribbed, blocky, and even square. Beefsteaks are large and meaty, with few seeds; oxhearts are large, aromatic, and heart shaped. You may also see types listed according to their use, such as slicing or paste tomatoes.

A large, black, shrunken area at the bottom of your tomatoes means blossom end rot has struck. This is caused by insufficient calcium reaching the developing tomato, usually because the plant didn't have enough water to carry the calcium to where it was needed during fruit development. By the time the black rot becomes noticeable, you will probably have forgotten about that hot day a few weeks back when all your tomato plants were drooping because they had dried out, especially as they soon picked up when you watered them. Once the damage has been done, there is no cure; however, the following tomatoes should not be affected, and the disorder is not contagious. Making sure plants never dry out will prevent blossom end rot from occurring.

Above: Once the tomatoes begin to ripen, check the plants at least every other day. If you find the skin splitting on some tomatoes, try picking them a day or two before they completely ripen, and let them ripen off the plant.

Pest patrol

You may need to protect the ripening tomatoes from birds by covering them with

Good eating

Store tomatoes at a cool room temperature; do not refrigerate them because this will ruin the flavor. If you have unripe tomatoes left on the plants when frost threatens, pick them and bring them indoors to ripen. Put them in an enclosed space, such as a drawer or a paper bag; those that have started to color will ripen over several weeks. You can speed up the process by putting a ripe apple or pear in with them. These fruits release ethylene gas, which ripens fruit, including tomatoes, quickly. You can use green tomatoes to make chutney. Or slice them, dip them in egg and bread crumbs, and fry them.

Cherry tomato **Plum tomato** **Beefsteak tomato**

Favorites

- **'Black Cherry'** Small, round, cherry-size tomatoes, an unusual deep purple-black. Good flavor and early cropping. Indeterminate.
- **'Bushsteak'** Large, meaty beefsteak tomatoes, but on a compact plant. Early to ripen, with a good flavor and perfect for small gardens. Bush.
- **'Early Girl'** Early, large tomatoes. Compact bush.
- **'Fourth of July'** An extra-early tomato, with rich-scarlet, medium fruit. Indeterminate.
- **'Fresh Salsa'** Plum tomatoes with few seeds. Bush.
- **'Honeybunch'** An early type, with red, currant-size tomatoes that are sweet and tasty. Indeterminate.
- **'Italian Ice'** Unusual, small tomatoes ripening from green to ivory white. Mild flavor. Indeterminate.
- **'Orange Blossom'** Medium to large, deep-orange tomatoes with a good texture and mild flavor. Early ripening. Bush.
- **'Oregon Spring'** Medium, early tomatoes. Ideal for cool areas. Bush.
- **'Patio Princess'** Small, compact plants ideal for pots and patio growing. Good crop of small to medium red tomatoes. Compact bush.
- **'Red Robin'** Compact type for small pots or hanging baskets, with scarlet cherry tomatoes. Compact bush.
- **'Sun Gold'** Golden-orange, cherry-size tomatoes with a sweet, full flavor. Indeterminate.
- **'Sweetheart of the Patio'** Compact plants with sweet, baby cherry tomatoes. Ideal for pots. Compact bush.
- **'Tigerella'** Early, with round, red tomatoes striped with orange-yellow. Indeterminate.
- **'Tomatoberry Garden'** Early type with heart-shaped tomatoes. Deep red, with a firm texture. Indeterminate.
- **'Tumbler'** Excellent for hanging baskets, producing a heavy crop of bright-red cherry tomatoes. Trailing bush.

Zucchini and other summer squash

Among the most prolific crops you can grow, zucchini and the other types of summer squash will liven up your garden and your table with their colorful crop in a range of interesting and unusual shapes. The more you pick, the more they will produce.

Sowing and transplanting

Zucchini and other summer squash love warm conditions and are sensitive to frost, but even so, they will grow well in most regions. Either sow them indoors in pots in midspring, or sow them directly outside in the ground after all risk of frost has passed. For sowing indoors, set two seeds in a 3½-inch (8cm) pot of seed-starting mix; cover with a propagator top; and keep in an evenly warm place. If both seeds germinate, remove the weakest seedling. Harden off young plants thoroughly before planting them outside when all risk of frost is over.

Alternatively, sow seeds outdoors in early summer. These plants like rich, moisture-retentive but free-draining soil, so prepare the soil well, adding plenty of well-rotted garden compost. Sow two or three seeds about 3 feet (1m) apart each way, and once the seedlings emerge, thin them to the strongest seedling. If you are planting transplants, also space them 3 feet (1m) apart.

Zucchini and summer squash need plenty of moisture, but the soil near the plants must drain freely to prevent the plant stems from rotting. Mound the soil for sowing or transplanting into a small hill so that water will drain away from the necks of the plants. At the same time, scoop out a shallow "moat" about 6 inches (15 cm) from the base of the hill, which will help retain moisture for the plant's roots.

Male vs. female flowers

Zucchini and summer squash produce separate male and female flowers, and the female flowers usually need to be pollinated to produce a crop. (You can tell female flowers from male flowers by a small swelling, which is the embryonic fruit, at the base of the female flower stem.) At the start of the flowering season, normally only male flowers are produced for a while. Once the female flowers start arriving, pollination can be delayed by cool weather, which discourages pollinating insects.

If necessary, you can lend a helping hand by picking a completely formed male flower, folding back the petals carefully, and inserting it into a female flower so that the male flower's pollen-covered anthers come into contact with the female's round, sticky stigma.

One or two varieties of squash have been bred to produce a parthenocarpic crop from unpollinated flowers. These are useful in areas with cool summers, where poor pollination is a common problem. They are also quick to produce a crop.

Care

Water the plants regularly, especially in dry spells. Adequate moisture is particularly important once flowering starts because it will encourage a good crop. If there is a cool spell after planting outdoors, cover the plants with cloches or floating row covers to keep them growing strongly.

Time to pick

Gather the vegetables when large enough to eat. For long types, 6 inches (15cm) is the ideal length; for round ones, 2–3 inches (5–7.5cm). Many squash types have prickly stems. If you have sensitive skin, wear long sleeves and gloves when working among the plants.

Opposite: Planting zucchini or summer squash through X-shaped cuts made into a sheet of black plastic will help keep the soil below moist, which is important for these plants.

Above: Use a sharp knife to cut zucchini and summer squash from the stem, leaving 1 inch (5cm) attached to the vegetable. If you have too many vegetables growing, small ones are ideal to use as baby vegetables.

Zucchini and other summer squash continued

Squash shapes

Zucchini: Long, slender, and cigar shaped, although there are a few spherical types.

Crookneck: Slender, curved tops, and a slightly bulbous base.

Straightneck: Like a crookneck but (obviously) minus the curve.

Patty pan: Flattened disk shape with a scalloped edge, somewhat like a flying saucer. Scallop squashes or scallopini are similar but with more depth.

Young zucchini and squash are more tender skinned and have a better texture than when they grow too large. Harvest them while they are small, which will also encourage the plant to concentrate its energies into producing more flowers. Check the plants daily, looking beneath the leafy canopy. It's easy to miss a squash and find it's turned into a monster a few days later.

Good eating

Summer squash will keep for a few days in a cool place, but they are best eaten as soon as possible after harvesting. If left for too long, they become flabby, and some become bitter.

You only need to trim off the ends of young squash before cooking or slicing raw into salads. If you have an overly large specimen, it is still edible. If a zucchini grows to 10 inches (25cm) or more, you will have an English "marrow." Cut it in half lengthwise, and scrape out the seedy, pithy center. If the skin is so tough that it cannot be pierced easily with a fingernail, peel it. The flesh can be cut into chunks and steamed until tender, or stuff the hollowed-out halves and bake in the oven.

Squash flowers make good eating, too. You can stuff them, or try dipping the blossoms in batter and deep-frying them. Make sure the flower centers are free of insects, and use the male flowers so that you don't sacrifice a potential vegetable.

Favorites

- **'Eight Ball'** Ball-shaped zucchini with a dark-green skin flecked with yellow on a bush plant.
- **'Flying Saucer'** Scalloped, deeply ribbed squash that are yellow with green tips.
- **'G-Star Hybrid'** Scallop-shaped, deep-green squash, quick to form on a compact plant. Recommended for southern and rainy climates.
- **'Onyx'** Glossy, deep-green zucchini; early cropping with a mild flavor. Compact bush plants.
- **'Parthenon'** F1 hybrid zucchini that produces parthenocarpic crop without pollination being necessary.
- **'Romanesco Latino'** A markedly ribbed zucchini that makes an attractive shape when cut across.
- **'Soleil'** Heavy crop of golden-yellow zucchini on vigorous plants; good resistance to powdery mildew.
- **'Spineless Beauty'** Deep-green zucchini flecked with yellow produced on an open plant. Spineless stems make harvesting easy and scratch free.
- **'Starship'** Dark-green, scallop-shaped squash on a vigorous bush.
- **'Sunburst'** Bright-yellow, deep patty pans or scallop squashes on an open-centered bush plant.
- **'Zephyr'** Firm, well-flavored crookneck variety. Mainly yellow but with a green tip. The depth of the green portion varies from plant to plant and season to season.

Zucchini

Ball-shaped zucchini

Crookneck squash

Scallop squash

Low-maintenance vegetables

These vegetables may not be speedy in their growth, but they are so easy to look after that you'll not have to spend much time caring for them—perfect for a busy lifestyle—and you'll have freshly picked vegetables through the winter months.

Garlic

Globe artichoke

A gourmet vegetable that is well worth growing for its stately, decorative appearance as well as its tasty flower buds, globe artichoke makes an impressive "architectural" addition to a flower border. Young plants are available from garden centers in spring. Plant outside after all risk of frost in a rich, moisture-retentive but free-draining soil. Choose a warm, sheltered site in full sun. Artichokes grow to 3–4 feet (1–1.2m) tall and need 3 feet (1m) of space in each direction. In mild areas with light frost (Zone 7 and above), you can grow artichokes as perennials. Protect the roots from cold by mulching the root area in winter. In cold regions, grow artichokes as annuals, and look for quick-maturing types, such as 'Imperial Star', 'Emerald', 'Tempo', and 'Violetto'.

Time to pick: Cut the heads when they are firm and plump, before the scales start to open. There will often be one or two smaller heads to follow from the main bud.

Garlic

This member of the onion family has a distinctive flavor. Peel off the papery skin of a garlic bulb to reveal separate cloves. Plant each of these to produce a new bulb. Plant in fall, before the first frost, in a sunny, sheltered position, in free-draining but reasonably fertile soil. Set the cloves upright, 3 inches (8cm) deep (slightly deeper in cold areas) and 6 inches (15cm) apart. Garlic also grows well in pots. There are two main types of garlic: softneck and hardneck. Hardneck is more cold tolerant, but does not store well. Obtain cloves, such as 'Bogatyr', 'Silver Rose', 'Purple Glazer', 'Silverskin', and 'Russian Red', from a specialty supplier.

Time to pick: When the leaves start to yellow and die back, garlic is ready for harvesting, usually in early summer. Let the bulbs dry in an airy place for two to four weeks. They should keep well for several months.

Globe artichoke

Horseradish

Jerusalem artichoke

It's not an artichoke and does not come from Jerusalem, but it is extremely easy to grow. This is a tall plant, at 10 feet (3m) or more, and it produces an abundance of knobbly tubers that taste similar to water chestnuts. Plant healthy tubers 4–6 inches (10–15cm) deep and 10–12 inches (25–30 cm) apart in a sunny position in free-draining soil. Be careful where you plant them. Every portion of tuber left in the soil will produce a new plant, so they can become invasive weeds. Because they grow so tall, make sure they are in a position where they will not shade other plants. Many suppliers sell unnamed types, but look for 'Fuseau' (red or white), which has smooth, nonknobbly roots that are easier to prepare. 'Stampede' is an early maturing type.

Time to pick: Dig up the tubers in fall and winter, being careful to remove as many as possible to limit the number of "volunteers" growing next year.

Horseradish

The vigorous, woody roots of horseradish are eye-wateringly pungent. Their white flesh makes a fiery, tangy sauce traditionally used to accompany beef, but horseradish also goes well with other meats and fish and sparks new life into coleslaw or dull mashed potatoes. Horseradish is easy to grow—so easy, in fact, that it needs to be confined or it will take over the yard. Obtain a section of root from a garden center (or a friend or neighbor) and plant it 4–6 inches (10–15cm) deep in early spring or fall. Growing it in a deep container of rich soil will prevent it from straying. The container can be sunk into the ground if you like. Keep moist in dry spells. Most roots are of unnamed types, but you may be able to find suppliers of 'Maliner Kren' and 'Big Top'.

Time to pick: Dig up the roots as required in fall or winter, saving some sections of root for replanting in the next season. Peel and grate small sections for use; if you think onions make your eyes water, wait until you have tried grating horseradish.

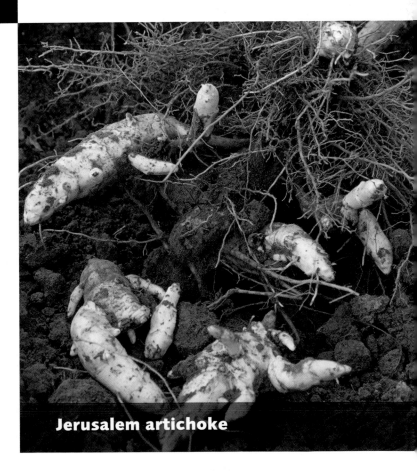

Jerusalem artichoke

Low-maintenance vegetables
continued

Leeks

If you are growing leeks as baby vegetables, leave a few in place to grow into full-size plants for winter. (See "Baby Leek," pages 116–117.) They are trouble free and will stand well through the cold weather. Grow them as you would baby leeks, but pull them in stages to leave plants for winter use at 6–8 inches (15–20cm) spacing. They need little care other than occasional weeding. Grow a completely hardy variety, such as 'Lancelot', 'Electra', or 'Bandit', for overwintering in cold regions.

Time to pick: Pull the plants as required right through the winter. In cold spells, leeks can become frozen into the ground, so lift a supply before the weather gets too bad; bundle them together; and half bury them in a large pot of light soil or potting mix.

Onions and shallots

Leeks

Onions and shallots

Although onions and shallots can be raised from seeds, it is much easier to grow them from sets, immature bulbs that continue to grow and develop once planted in soil. Prepare the soil thoroughly, and plant the sets 3–4 inches (8–10cm) apart in early spring. The tip of the set should just be showing above soil level. Cut off any lengths of dead leaf—birds sometimes use these to pull the sets out of the ground. Keep the plants weeded throughout the growing season. Look for heat-treated sets, which will not bolt to seed. Onion 'Stuttgarter' is an old favorite, while 'Forum' is early ripening, and 'Walla Walla' is exceptionally large. 'Pikant' is a reliable shallot.

Time to pick: Lift the bulbs in early fall as they become large enough or when the tops start to dry and fall over. Use onions and shallots grown from sets as soon as possible after lifting because they may not store well; however, you can keep completely ripe, dry bulbs for a few weeks in a cool, dark place. You'll need about 10 days to dry the onions in a well-ventilated area.

Parsnip

Although parsnips need a long growing season—they are a winter crop—they will produce a good crop of sweet-tasting roots all through the season. Sow parsnip seeds early in spring, spacing groups of two or three seeds 4–6 in (10–15cm) apart. The soil needs to be deeply cultivated to prevent the roots from becoming forked and stunted. Seeds take a long time to germinate, so you can sow quick-growing vegetables, such as radishes, between the parsnip seeds to use garden space efficiently. You'll harvest the quick-growing crop before the parsnips need the space. Once the parsnip seedlings appear, thin them to the strongest seedling. 'Gladiator' is a good-quality F1 hybrid. 'All American' and 'Hollow Crown' are two other popular parsnip choices.

Time to pick: Waiting for the first fall frost will improve the flavor of the roots. Dig roots up as you need them throughout the winter.

Rhubarb

Parsnip

Rhubarb

The leaf stems of rhubarb, cooked with sugar as a dessert, are a spring treat, and the plant, once established, needs virtually no care. It does need space but is a bold and decorative addition to the yard. Buy rhubarb crowns from garden centers or mail-order suppliers, and plant in spring in an open, sunny position so that the buds are 1–2 inches (3–5cm) below the soil surface. Allow at least 2 feet (60cm) of space each way. Rhubarb can continue to crop for over 10 years, so take the time to prepare the soil thoroughly before planting, adding plenty of organic matter; the soil must be free draining. Rhubarb is a cool-season plant, but in hot southern areas you can grow it from seeds as an annual, sowing in late summer and harvesting in spring. 'Valentine', with sweet, red stalks, is a vigorous plant in cold areas.

Time to pick: Try to resist pulling any stems in the first season of a perennial planting. On established plants, pull or cut the stems in spring as soon as they are large enough. Don't sample the leaves—they are poisonous.

Glossary

Blanching
Protecting parts of a crop, such as leeks, from light to make the growth pale and tender; or heat treating vegetables by boiling them before freezing them to improve their storage quality.

Bolting
Premature flowering and seeding of a crop, which often makes it useless for eating.

Broadcast
To scatter seeds or fertilizer over an area randomly, instead of in rows.

Bulb
Plant storage organ formed from a modified stem.

Calyx
The sepals or outer part of a flower that sometimes remain on the fruit or vegetable, such as a strawberry or tomato.

Check
A temporary interruption to the growth of a plant often caused by cold conditions or disturbance, such as transplanting.

Cloche
A temporary, movable covering used to protect plants from adverse weather or to warm the soil.

Clove
Segment of a garlic bulb.

Crown
The part of a plant where the stems join the roots, usually at soil level.

Cultivar
Short for "cultivated variety," a plant variety that has been created or selected and maintained through cultivation.

Cut-and-come-again
A plant that is harvested over a period of time without uprooting it; for example, some lettuce are picked leaf by leaf.

Day length
The number of hours of daylight per day, which sometimes determines the flowering and cropping season of plants.

Dibble
Pointed tool used to make planting holes in the soil.

Ericaceous
Plants, such as blueberries, that will not tolerate lime in the soil; also the lime-free potting mix used to grow such plants.

F1 hybrid
The first generation of a variety bred from a deliberate cross between two different named varieties. These usually give heavier, more uniform crops. Seeds from F1 hybrids will not breed true; that is, they will not have the same characteristics as the parent plant.

Fallow
An area of ground left deliberately uncultivated.

Farmyard manure
Waste products from farm animals used (when rotted) as a soil amendment.

Fingerling
A type of potato prized for its flavor, with long, slender, often bunched tubers that resemble fingers.

Floating row cover
Lightweight synthetic fabric that can be laid over a crop to protect it from pests or extremes of temperature.

Growing point
The tip of a shoot where cells divide to extend the growth.

Harden off
The method of gradually acclimating plants raised under protection to cooler conditions outside before planting them in the ground.

Hardy
Able to survive cold winters outside without protection.

Herb
A plant with aromatic foliage, used in dishes as a flavoring.

Hilling
Mounding up soil around the base of a plant, often to help drain water away from the neck of the plant.

Hybrid
The product of a cross between two different plant varieties.

Leaf mold
Decomposed leaves, used as a soil amendment.

Mature
A plant that has reached the final stage of its development, or (more loosely for gardeners) is producing a harvestable crop.

Microclimate
A local climate within a small area that may differ from the more general climate surrounding it.

Microgreens
Vegetables grown for harvesting (without their roots) as very young seedlings.

Midrib
The central vein of a leaf, sometimes large and prominent, such as in Swiss chard.

Moisture-retentive
Growing material that is capable of holding a good supply of moisture that is accessible to plants without making them waterlogged.

Monogerm
Beet seeds in which the normal clusters of several seeds have been reduced to a single seed so that less thinning of seedlings is necessary.

Mulch
A layer of material, such as garden compost, bark chips, or black plastic sheet, spread over the soil to keep in moisture and warmth and prevent weed growth.

NPK
The major plant nutrients, nitrogen, phosphorus, and potassium, which are found in combination or singly in many plant fertilizers.

Organic
A system of growing plants without using artificial chemicals.

Organic matter
Decomposed or decomposing material derived from something that has once lived—for example, leaf mold, manure, garden compost—used as a soil amendment.

Parthenocarpic
Fruit produced without fertilization, such as occurs with some types of zucchini.

Pelleted seed
A seed that has been covered with an inert claylike material to make it easier to handle.

Pesticide
A substance used for killing pests. Pesticides may be artificial or organic.

pH
A scale used for measuring the alkalinity and acidity of soil: pH 7 is neutral; above pH 7 is alkaline; and below pH 7 is acidic.

Propagator
Equipment used for raising seeds or cuttings, providing a protected, humid atmosphere, sometimes with heating.

Raised bed
A bed of soil with an edging of stones, bricks, planks, and the like that is raised above ground level.

Root hairs
The tiny hairlike projections along the tips of roots that are responsible for absorbing water and minerals from the soil.

Root-ball
The mass of roots together with the soil clinging to them when a plant is lifted from the soil or removed from its container.

Root-bound
A plant that has been growing for so long in a small pot that the pot is completely filled with roots; the plant's development will be checked.

Rose
A pierced plastic or metal fitting for the end of a hose or spout of a watering can that breaks up the supplied water into small droplets.

Runners
Specialized stems, as in a strawberry, that grow along the ground, producing roots and shoots that will form new plants from nodes along their length.

Scoville units
A measure of the heat found in peppers and chilies.

Seed leaves
The first leaves (also called "cotyledons") that form on a seedling, often different in shape and size from the true leaves that follow them.

Seedbed
An area of soil specially prepared for sowing seeds.

Seedling
A young plant when it first emerges from the seed.

Soaker hose
A perforated hose that can be laid alongside plants to provide a gentle supply of water near the roots. Also called a seep hose or trickle hose.

Soilless
Growing mix that does not contain loam (soil). Generally based on peat or other substances such as composted bark or cocoa shell.

Spray gun
An attachment for a hose that breaks water up into a range of different patterns to apply to plants.

Stringless
Bean types that are bred to be without tough, stringy edges to the pods, making preparation quicker and easier.

Temperate
Regions where the climate is moderate and without extremes, having mild to warm summers and cool winters.

Tender
Plant unable to withstand cold weather.

Tendrils
Slender shoots, as on peas, that twine around objects to help support the plant.

Thinning
Reducing the number of seedlings to give the remaining plants more room to grow.

Trace elements
Plant nutrients needed in very small quantities; certain symptoms, such as the yellowing of leaf veins, will be obvious when trace elements are in short supply.

Transplant
To move a plant to a new position, often from a pot or tray to a bed outside.

Tuber
A modified stem forming an underground plant storage organ, as in a potato or Jerusalem artichoke.

Water-retaining granules
Granules of polymer that absorb many times their own weight in water. When mixed with soil, they retain water for plants to use so that less frequent watering is necessary.

Seed and plant suppliers

United States

American Meadows Inc.
223 Avenue D, Ste. 30
Williston, VT 05495
www.americanmeadows.com

W. Atlee Burpee & Co.
300 Park Ave.
Warminster, PA 18974
www.burpee.com

Bountiful Gardens
18001 Shafer Ranch Rd.
Willits, CA 95490
www.bountifulgardens.org

L. E. Cooke Co.
26333 Road 140
Visalia, CA 93292
www.lecooke.com

The Cooks' Garden
P.O. Box C5030
Warminster, PA 18974
www.cooksgarden.com

Daisy Farm
Hwy. M-152
Dowagiac, MI 49047
www.daisyfarms.net

DiMeo Blueberry Farms
366 Middle Rd.
Hammonton, NJ 08037
www.dimeofarms.com

Egyptian Walking Onion
301 S. 10th St.
Garfield, WA 99130
www.egyptianwalkingonion.com

Evergreen Y. H. Enterprises
P.O. Box 17538
Anaheim, CA 92817
www.evergreenseeds.com

Henry Field's Seed & Nursery Co.
P.O. Box 397
Aurora, IN 47001–0397
www.henryfields.com

Fall Creek Farm and Nursery
39318 Jasper Lowell Rd.
Lowell, OR 97452
www.fallcreeknursery.com

Goodwin Creek Gardens
P.O. Box 83
Williams, OR 97544
www.goodwincreekgardens.com

Gourmet Seed International
HC 12 Box 510
Tatum, NM 88267–9700
www.gourmetseed.com

Gurney's Seed & Nursery Co.
P.O. Box 4178
Greendale, IN 47025–4178
www.gurneys.com

Harris Seeds
P.O. Box 24966
Rochester, NY 14624–0966
www.harrisseeds.com

Hartmann's Plant Co.
P.O. Box 100
Locata, MI 49063–0100
www.hartmannsplantcompany.com

Heirloom Acres Seeds
2529 CR 338
New Bloomfield, MO 65063
www.heirloomacresseeds.com

High Mowing Organic Seeds
76 Quarry Rd.
Wolcott, VT 05680
www.highmowingseeds.com

Indiana Berry & Plant Co.
5218 W. 500 S.
Huntingburg, IN 47542
www.inberry.com

Irish Eyes Garden Seeds
5045 Robinson Canyon Rd.
Ellensburg, WA 98926
www.irisheyesgardenseeds.com

Italian Seed and Tool Co.
HC 12 Box 510
Tatum, NM 88267–9700
www.italianseedandtool.com

Johnny's Selected Seeds
955 Benton Ave.
Winslow, ME 03901–2601
www.johnnyseeds.com

Nichols Garden Nursery
1190 Old Salem Rd. NE
Albany, OR 97321
www.nicholsgardennursery.com

Nourse Farms Inc.
41 River Rd.
Whately, MA 01373
www.noursefarms.com

Oikos Tree Crop
P.O. Box 19425
Kalamazoo, MI 40019–0425
www.oikostreecrops.com

One Green World
28696 S. Cramer Rd.
Molalla, OR 97038–8576
www.onegreenworld.com

Park Seed Co.
1 Parkton Ave.
Greenwood, SC 29647
www.parkseed.com

**Peaceful Valley Farm
& Garden Supply**
P.O. Box 2209
Grass Valley, CA 95945
www.groworganic.com

Raintree Nursery
391 Butts Rd.
Morton, WA 98356
www.raintreenursery.com

Reimer Seeds
P.O. Box 236
Mount Holly, NC 28120–0236
www.reimerseeds.com

Renee's Garden Seeds
6060A Graham Hill Rd.
Felton, CA 95018
www.reneesgarden.com

Sandy Mush Herb Nursery
316 Surrett Cove Rd.
Leicester, NC 28748
www.sandymushherbs.com

St. Lawrence Nurseries
325 State Hwy. 345
Potsdam, NY 13676
www.sln.potsdam.ny.us

Seed Savers Exchange
3094 N. Winn Rd.
Decorah, IA 52101
www.seedsavers.org

Sproutpeople
170 Mendell St.
San Francisco, CA 94124
www.sproutpeople.com

Stokes Seed
P.O. Box 548
Buffalo, NY 14240–0548
www.stokeseeds.com

Sustainable Seed Co.
P.O. Box 636
Petaluma, CA 94952
www.sustainableseedco.com

Territorial Seed Co.
P.O. Box 158
Cottage Grove, OR 97424
www.territorialseed.com

**Thompson & Morgan
Seedsmen Inc.**
P.O. Box 4086
Lawrenceburg, IN 47025
www.tmseeds.com

Tomato Growers Supply Co.
P.O. Box 60015
Fort Myers, FL 33906
www.tomatogrowers.com

Totally Tomatoes
334 W. Stroud St.
Randolph, WI 53956
www.totallytomatoes.com

Vegetable Seed Warehouse
10234 Lavonia Hwy.
Carnesville, GA 30521
www.vegetableseedwarehouse.com

Vermont Bean Seed Co.
334 W. Stroud St.
Randolph, WI 53956
www.vermontbean.com

Veseys Seed
P.O. Box 9000
Calais, ME 04619–6102
www.veseys.com

Victory Seed Co.
P.O. Box 192
Molalla, OR 97038
www.victoryseeds.com

Waters Blueberry Farm
915 Bainbridge Rd.
Smithville, MO 64089
www.watersblueberryfarm.com

Well-Sweep Herb Farm
205 Mount Bethel Rd.
Port Murray, NJ 07865–4147
www.wellsweep.com

Canada

William Dam Seeds Ltd.
279 Hwy 8
R.R. 1 Dundas, ON L9H 5E1
www.damseeds.ca

Dominion Seed House
P.O. Box 2500
Georgetown, ON L7G 5L6
www.dominion-seed-house.com

Halifax Seed Co. Inc.
5860 Kane St.
P.O. Box 8026, Stn A
Halifax NS B3K 5L8
www.halifaxseed.ca

McFayden Seed Co.
1000 Parker Blvd.
Brandon, MB R7A 6N4
www-secure.mcfayden.com

Strawberry Tyme Farms Inc.
R.R. 2
Simcoe, ON N3Y 4K1
www.strawberrytyme.com

Vesey's Seeds
P.O. Box 9000
Charlottetown, PE C1A 8K6
www.veseys.com/ca/en

Index

Page numbers in **bold** refer to entries in the "Directory of Food Crops," pages 78–167.

Index

Photo credits/acknowledgments

Front cover: Photolibrary/Photoalto/Laurence Mouton (TR); Photolibrary/Friedrich Strauss (ML); Photolibrary/Mike Grandmaison (BL); Photolibrary/Gary K. Smith.

Alamy: Neil Holmes 7; Nick Hanna 10 (TR); Rob Cousins 15 (T); Ros Drinkwater 23 (T); Gary Smith 61 (BR); Ottmar Diez 64 (ML); ArtMediaPix 127 (MR).

Ian Armitage: 27 (B); 57 (T); 79 (1) (2); 81; 82; 94 (L); 96; 118 (B); 157 (B).

T C Bird: 5; 10 (BL); 16–17; 18 (B); 19 (TL); 19 (BL); 20 (TL and BC); 28 (TR); 40; 42–43; 58 (BL); 62 (TR); 100; 102 (6); 114; 130 (B); 146 (B); 147 (B); 154; 156–157; 160.

Corbis: Mark Bolton 16 (MR); Mark Bolton 24 (BR); Bilic 71.

Jane Courtier: 25 (B); 41 (TR); 59; 102 (11); 116; 131 (R); 145 (L); 146 (B).

Dreamstime: Argument 66 (TR); Bedo 68; 79(3); 84; 127 (TR).

GAP photos: 79 (7); 80 (BL); 90–91. Freidrich Strauss 2; 8; 11 (TR); 20–21; 21 (BR); 24–25; 47 (BR); 124 (BL). FhF Greenmedia 14 (TR); 58 (TR); 79 (6); 88. Bios 15 (BL); 167 (BL). Graham Strong 18 (TL); 19 (R); 104. Victoria Firmston 24 (L); 24–25. Elke Borkowski 26; 28 (L); 37; 95; 150–151. Mark Bolton 27 (T); 29; 163 (2). Michael King 28 (BR); 50–51. Howard Rice 32 (L); 46. BBC Magazines Ltd. 39 (TR); 119. Yvonne Innes and Olivia Harrison 52. Maayke de Ridder 55. Jo Whitworth 79 (8) (9); 94; 97; 80 (BL); 88; 89; 90; 91; 94 (L); 164 (L). Maxine Adcock 89. Juliette Wade 79 (11); 100–101; 102 (9); 123; 136 (R); 167 (R). Paul Debois 103 (10); 124 (TR). Graham Strong 104. Geoff Kidd 125. Julia Boulton 129 (T). Sharon Pearson 131 (L). Maddie Thornhill 132. Martin Hughes-Jones 153 (3). Howard Rice 165 (L). Nicola Browne 165 (R). Richard Bloom 167 (L).

Harris Seeds: 163 (3).

Haxnicks Ltd.: 63.

Home Grown Revolution/www.homegrownrev.co.uk: Rosy Stamp 75 (TR).

Clive Nichols: 6.

Photolibrary: Creativ Studio Heinemann 9; Garden Picture Library 11 (B). David Burton 14 (L). Ron Evans 17 (R). Gary K. Smith 21; 47 (TL); 72–73; 126; 138 (3); 144. Andrea Jones 22 (TR); 102 (1); 105 (BR); 122. Lynn Keddie 22 (BR and ML). Clive Nichols 23 (B). Kate Gadsby 30–31. FoodCollection 31 (BL); 73 (BL). Leroy Alfonse 32–33. Weill Rachel 45. Pernilla Bergdahl 47 (TR). Freidrich Strauss 47 (BR). Mark Winwood 62 (BR). Stephen Hamilton 67. Clare Parker 69. Annette Hempfling 102 (2); 107 (BL). Kurt Mobus 102 (5); 113. Creativ Studio Heinemann 103 (BL). Herbert Kehrer 121 (4). Lucy Mason 127 (BR). Mike Grandmaison 140 (TR). Ulrich Niehoff 148 (B).

Denis Ryan: 60; 61 (TL).

Shutterstock: 1; Marek Pawluczuk 36. LianeM 41 (BR). Tereza Dvorak 51 (L). ER_09 51 (M). N. Mitchell 51 (R). Marekuliasz 56 (B). Palto 65; 66 (BL). Nagy-Bagoly Arpad 74–75. Lilyana Vynogradova 80 (BR); 92(3) (6); 102 (13); 103 (14); 136 (L); 121 (2); 121 (3); 129 (B); 130 (TL); 134; 138 (5); 153 (1), (4); 164 (R).

Suffolk Herbs: 79 (5); 87.

Thompson Morgan: 79 (10); 98; 83; 92 (1) (4); 98–99.

Mark Winwood: 13; 38; 39 (TL and BL); 41 (TL and MM); 42; 44; 48; 49; 50; 56 (TR); 57 (CR); 76–77; 78, 96–97; 79(4); 86; 92 (2); 102 (3) (4) (7) (8) (12); 105 (TL); 106; 108, 110; 111; 112–113; 117; 118 (T); 121 (1); 128; 133; 135; 137; 138 (1), (2), (4), (6), (7), (8); 140 (ML); 142–143, 159, (7) (8), 166 (R); 145 (R); 146 (T); 147 (T); 148 (T); 149; 150 (L); 151 (R); 153 (2); 156 (L); 158–159; 161; 163 (1) (4); 166 (R).

ARTWORK

U. S. Department of Agriculture: 34 and 35.

ACKNOWLEDGMENTS

The author and Toucan Books would like to thank the following people for their assistance: Ian Armitage; Sarah Bebbington; Sophie Courtier; Steve and Jill Cox; Gayla Duval; The Green Street Green Allotment Society; Gaynor Egan and Sean Gilbert of Home Grown Revolution; and Jon Kemp and the staff at Notcutts Garden Centre, Maidstone, Kent.

Have a gardening, decorating, or home improvement project?
Look for these and other fine Creative Homeowner books wherever books are sold

1001 IDEAS FOR BETTER GARDENING

Tips on gardening methods and selecting plants for your landscape.

Over 450 photographs and illustrations.
256 pp.
8½" x 10⅞"
$24.95 (US)
$27.95 (CAN)
BOOK #: CH274183

COMPLETE HOUSEPLANTS

Secrets to growing the most popular types of houseplants.

Over 480 photographs and illustrations.
224 pp.
9" x 10"
$19.95 (US)
$21.95 (CAN)
BOOK #: CH274820

3 STEP VEGETABLE GARDENING

A quick and easy guide for growing your own fruit and vegetables.

Over 300 photographs.
224 pp.
8½" x 10⅞"
$19.95 (US)
$21.95 (CAN)
BOOK #: CH274557

SUCCESSFUL CONTAINER GARDENING

Information to grow your own flower, fruit, and vegetable "gardens."

Over 240 photographs.
160 pp.
8½" x 10⅞"
$14.95 (US)
$17.95 (CAN)
BOOK #: CH274857

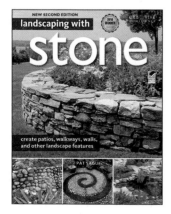

LANDSCAPING WITH STONE

Ideas for incorporating stone into the landscape.

Over 335 photographs.
224 pp.
8½" x 10⅞"
$19.95 (US)
$21.95 (CAN)
BOOK #: CH274179

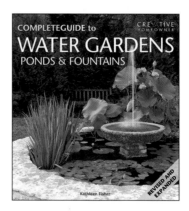

COMPLETE GUIDE TO WATER GARDENS, PONDS & FOUNTAINS

Secrets to creating garden water features.

Over 600 photographs and illustrations.
240 pp.
9" x 10"
$19.95 (US)
$21.95 (CAN)
BOOK #: CH274458

For more information and to order direct, go to **www.creativehomeowner.com**